Elevator ESSEntials

How to Create an Effective Elevator Pitch

Chris O'Leary

"From Chris's mouth to God's ears. If only entrepreneurs would follow Chris's advice, I wouldn't be losing my hearing and I would have more time to play hockey." – *Guy Kawasaki*

Copyright © 2008 by Chris O'Leary, all rights reserved

No part of this book may be reproduced, stored in a retrieval system, or transmitted, in any form or by any means, except for brief excerpts for the purpose of review, without written permission of the author.

ISBN-10: 0-9727479-1-5
ISBN-13: 978-0-9727479-1-2

First Edition: September 2008, Version 1.0

FOR LAURA

FOR MORE INFORMATION

Chris O'Leary offers a wide range of services aimed at helping individuals and organizations improve their elevator pitch...

Elevator Pitch Reviews, Tune-Ups, and Writing
Sales Training
Consulting
Speaking

To find out how to contact Chris O'Leary, to get more information about Chris O'Leary and the services he provides, or to learn about volume discounts that are available for this book, please go to...

www.ElevatorPitchEssentials.com

TABLE OF CONTENTS

1. **Executive Summary** 1
2. **Elevator Pitch 101** 4
3. **Sample Elevator Pitches** 12
   - 3.1. SalesLogix 13
   - 3.2. Elevator Pitch Essentials 19
   - 3.3. Personal Elevator Pitch 23
4. **The Nine C's** 27
   - 4.1. Concise 28
   - 4.2. Clear 35
   - 4.3. Compelling 43
   - 4.4. Credible 47
   - 4.5. Conceptual 53
   - 4.6. Concrete 57
   - 4.7. Consistent 61
   - 4.8. Customized 68
   - 4.9. Conversational 75
5. **Frequently Made Mistakes** 78
6. **Before's and After's** 86
   - 6.1. CareCoordinator 87
   - 6.2. Novel Imaging 91
   - 6.3. Rogue Research 96
7. **Coda**
   - Recommended Reading 99
   - Acknowledgements 99
   - Endnotes 100

Summary Sentence

The Customer
The Problem
The Pain
The Competition
The Solution
The Features
The Benefits
The Team
The Objective

The Deal
The Technology

1. EXECUTIVE SUMMARY

> *"Brevity is the soul of wit."*
> – WIlliam Shakespeare

It doesn't matter what you are selling; maybe it's an idea for a new business, an existing product or service, or a project. It also doesn't matter who you are selling it to; maybe they are an investor, a potential customer, or a potential client. In order to have a chance of closing the deal, you first need the audience to listen to what you have to say.

Unfortunately, few people realize that getting the audience to listen to what you have to say is much harder than it looks.

The problem is that people are busy. Just like you, they have too much to do and too little time to get it all done. What's more, it never fails that the more potentially helpful someone is, the busier they are likely to be. If you want to be successful, you need to take this problem seriously; you need to figure out how to communicate your message in a way that will catch the attention of someone who has 17 other things on their mind.

You need an elevator pitch.

An elevator pitch is an overview of an idea, product, service, project, person, or other Solution to a problem and is designed to just get a conversation started. An elevator pitch is designed to quickly catch the attention of the audience, persuade them to pay attention to what you have to say, and convince them that they want to hear more. An elevator pitch does this by answering basic – but all too often overlooked – questions like…

- **What** is it?
- **Who** needs it?
- **Why** do they need it?
- **WhoRU** to see the problem and to build the solution?

Just as importantly, an effective elevator pitch leaves for later the details about HOW your Solution works.

> **Elevator Pitch:** An elevator pitch is an overview of an idea, product, service, project, person, or other Solution to a problem and is designed to just get a conversation started.

PEOPLE ARE BUSY

Just like you, people are busy; they have too many things to do and too little time to get them all done. What's more, it never fails that the more potentially helpful someone is, the busier they are likely to be.

YOU ARE DIFFERENT

The audience is unlikely to be as interested in, or as knowledgeable about, your Solution as you are. As a result, you must ease them into it.

THE NINE C'S

1. **Concise** – An effective elevator pitch contains as few words as possible, but no fewer (and no more than 250 words).

2. **Clear** – Rather than being filled with acronyms, MBA-speak, and ten-dollar words, an effective elevator pitch can be understood by your grandparents, your spouse, and your children.

3. **Compelling** – An effective elevator pitch explains the problem your Solution solves.

4. **Credible** – An effective elevator pitch explains why you are qualified to see the problem and to build the solution.

5. **Conceptual** – An effective elevator pitch stays at a fairly high level and does not go into too much unnecessary detail.

6. **Concrete** – As much as is possible, an effective elevator pitch is also specific and tangible.

7. **Consistent** – Every version of an elevator pitch conveys the same basic message.

8. **Customized** – An effective elevator pitch addresses the specific interests and concerns of the audience.

9. **Conversational** – An effective elevator pitch is designed to just start a conversation with the audience.

GO EASY ON THE HYPE

While it is important to appear enthusiastic and confident, you do not want to look naïve or, worst of all, make your Solution sound too good to be true.

DON'T GET LOST IN THE HOW

Instead of focusing on the topic you love and are the most comfortable talking about – HOW your Solution works – you must first answer more basic questions like "WHAT is it?", "WHO needs it?", "WHY do they need it?", and "WHORU to see the problem and build the solution?"

START WITH A SUMMARY SENTENCE

When you first start talking to someone, it is critically important that you make a good first impression and set the stage for a more detailed discussion of your Solution. The way to do that is to begin your elevator pitch with a summary sentence of 25 words or less. Below is a template that I have found to be very effective for structuring a summary sentence.

> COMPANY NAME is a TYPE OF COMPANY and has developed a PRODUCT CATEGORY that is KEY BENEFIT(S) than existing solutions (like CHIEF COMPETITORS).

EXPLAIN WHAT'S WRONG WITH THE STATE OF THE ART

Experienced investors won't back a Solution In Search Of A Problem (SISOAP), so you must be sure to explain what will drive people to change and adopt your Solution.

MEMORIZE IT & REHEARSE IT

Because you will use your elevator pitch everywhere, you should memorize it and rehearse it. That will ensure that people receive a consistent message. It will also help you look and feel more confident.

LISTEN TO THE AUDIENCE

When delivering an elevator pitch, listening is just as important as talking. One way to judge the effectiveness of your elevator pitch is to pay attention to the first question the audience asks.

2. ELEVATOR PITCH 101

> *"He that has no silver in his purse should have silver on his tongue."*
> – Thomas Fuller

Picture this. You're an entrepreneur and are attending an emerging technology conference in a swanky hotel. You're there to learn something about the world of venture capital and make a few contacts. At the end of the day, you decide to change clothes before going out for the night. You head over to the elevator bank, push the "Up" button, and step through the doors of a waiting elevator car. Just as the doors begin to close, you hear a voice shout out, "Hold the door, please." You swing your notepad between the closing doors and, as the doors bounce back, through the opening bounds a 40-something woman who just happens to be one of the country's top venture capitalists.

Or maybe you're a salesperson and have spent the last year penetrating an account. The client is ready to buy, but everything is being held up by your contact's inability to get the approval of his V.P. After attending yet another status meeting, you step into an elevator to go down to your car. You notice that the other person in the elevator is your contact's V.P.

Or maybe you're a project champion in a large company and you have just come up with an idea that will save – or better yet make – your company millions of dollars a year. After giving yet another presentation and getting yet another set of maybe's, you get in the elevator to go back up to your office. As you step through the doors, you notice the CEO of your company standing on your left.

In each case, what would you do?

THE PROBLEM

While the scenes I paint above may seem a bit idyllic, encounters like them happen every day to entrepreneurs, inventors, salespeople, project champions, authors, screenwriters, job seekers, and others.

By virtue of design, connections, or luck, they come face to face with the person who can help them achieve their goal; who can help them sell their Solution, regardless of whether that Solution is an idea, product, service, project, book, script, or themselves.

The problem is that too few people are prepared to deal with such a situation.

They haven't considered what they would do, much less prepared something to say or rehearsed saying it. As a result, instead of capitalizing on the opportunity, they just let it walk out the door.

THE SOLUTION

The goal of this book is to ensure that you know how to handle situations like the ones I describe above; to ensure that you know what to do, and what to say, if you have just a minute or two to catch the attention of the person with whom you most need to speak.

That means developing an elevator pitch.

Before I get into the specifics of what makes an elevator pitch effective, let me first take one of the lessons of this book to heart and give you an overview of what an elevator pitch is and why you need one.

What Exactly is an Elevator Pitch? – An elevator pitch is several things. Of course, an elevator pitch is a communication tool; it will help you articulate your message. An elevator pitch is also a sales tool; it will help you raise the money, and close the deals, that you need to be successful.

However, and most importantly, an elevator pitch is a teaching tool.

While it is of course important that you eventually close the deal, there is no point in trying to close the deal if the audience does not understand what you are talking about and why they should care.

As a result, an elevator pitch is designed to play the role of a primer; a high-level and basic introduction to whatever it is that you are selling.

An effective elevator pitch is designed to give the audience just enough information that they have a sense of what you are talking about and want to know more. Just as importantly, an effective elevator pitch is designed to not give the audience so much information that they feel overwhelmed and tune you out.

Think drinking fountain, not fire hose.

If you are going to be successful, you have to ease the audience into your Solution; you have to give them a chance to catch up to you and all the thinking you have done over the past months or years.

Why do You Need an Elevator Pitch? – While you no doubt love, are fascinated by, and are passionate about what you are doing, and could spend hours talking about it, most people aren't like you.

In all likelihood, when it comes to the people whose help you will need to bring your Solution to life, they aren't going to be nearly as knowledgeable about, or as interested in, your Solution as you are. As a result, they are unlikely to appreciate – or even notice – the intricacies, subtleties, and details of it. Instead, they will only understand and – initially at least – be interested in the big picture.

Even if they do share your interest in and knowledge of your field, it never fails that the more potentially helpful a person is, the busier they are likely to be.

Just like you, they have too many things to do and too little time to get them all done. That means they must constantly – and quickly – decide what to pay attention to and what to ignore.

As a result, you must come up with a way of explaining your Solution that will grab the attention of someone who has 17 other things on their mind. You must assume that people are looking for a reason to tune you out, not that they want to hear what you have to say. You must explain your idea in a manner that requires the audience to do the least amount of work.

Above all else, you must get to the point.

Only by doing that will you get the attention of the audience and have a chance of getting into the details of what it is that you are selling.

A DEFINITION

Now that I've given you a high-level overview – or in other words an elevator pitch – of what an elevator pitch is and why you need one, let me give you a short definition of an elevator pitch...

> *An elevator pitch is an overview of an idea, product, service, project, person, or other Solution to a problem and is designed to just get a conversation started.*

While that definition is relatively self-explanatory, let me take a moment to discuss what the most important of those words mean.

Overview – The point of an elevator pitch isn't to get into every detail of your Solution. Instead, all you want to do – and all you have time to do – is to make sure the audience understands what you are talking about, and what's in it for them, at a fairly high level.

Getting into the details of your Solution during your elevator pitch will only confuse people.

Idea, Service, Project, Person or Solution – While the term "Elevator Pitch" is typically used in the context of entrepreneurship – and in particular in selling ideas for new businesses to venture capitalists and angel investors – the truth is that the idea can be applied to a wide variety of contexts. A good elevator pitch is an essential tool for a salesperson, a person trying to sell a project to their boss, or for someone who is looking for a job.

Just Get a Conversation Started – One reason why so many people deliver poor elevator pitches – and why so many elevator pitches are too long and/or too detailed – is that they don't understand the purpose of an elevator pitch. They assume the purpose of an elevator pitch is to close the deal while in truth the purpose of an elevator pitch is to just interest the audience in continuing to talk.

No more, and no less.

THE NINE C'S

Now that you have a high-level sense of what an elevator pitch is, and what an elevator pitch is designed to do, let me drop down a level and discuss the characteristics of an effective elevator pitch.

After working with many would-be entrepreneurs, and studying hundreds of effective and ineffective elevator pitches, I have found that effective elevator pitches tend to be nine things...

1. **Concise**
2. **Clear**
3. **Compelling**
4. **Credible**
5. **Conceptual**
6. **Concrete**
7. **Consistent**
8. **Customized**
9. **Conversational**

I discuss each of The Nine C's at length elsewhere, but in the interests of repetition – and I have found that repetition is good – let me give you quick sense of what I mean.

1. CONCISE

An effective elevator pitch contains as few words as possible, but no fewer (and no more than 250 words).

While many people say that an elevator pitch must be short to be effective, the truth is that it depends. Sometimes you only have a few seconds to get your point across. In situations like those, your elevator pitch must be extremely short. However, in other cases – such as the elevator pitch competitions that are hosted by many schools and organizations – you have considerably more time to convey your message. Often, that may be as much as one or two minutes.

While you do not want to go long, you also do not want to waste any of the precious time you have been given.

2. CLEAR

Rather than being filled with acronyms, MBA-speak, and ten-dollar words, an effective elevator pitch can be understood by your grandparents, your spouse, and your children.

This runs counter to what many people have learned in their academic and/or professional lives; that the way to impress people is to show them how smart you are by speaking in the elaborate, coded language of your field.

While that approach certainly works in some settings, it doesn't work when it comes to delivering an elevator pitch. Venture capitalists, angel investors, and executives are too experienced, and too busy, to want to deal with those kinds of games.

Instead, they just want you to speak English.

3. COMPELLING

An effective elevator pitch explains the problem your Solution solves.

In the world today there is this idea going around that people should never talk about problems and the pain they cause; that they should instead be "positive" and only talk about opportunities. The promise is that by focusing on the positive, only good things will happen. Conversely, we are warned that by focusing on pain, problems, and other "negative" things, only bad things will come to pass.

While that idea is of questionable merit in general, it is completely wrong when it comes to entrepreneurship and innovation.

If you study the lives and stories of successful entrepreneurs, intrapraneurs, and innovators, you will find that most are unabashed – and often serial – problem solvers.

They make their fortunes by finding, and then solving, good problems.

The same thing is true of the venture capitalists, angel investors, and executives who back them. They are constantly on the lookout for people who understand the importance of finding, and then solving, good problems. As a result, an effective elevator pitch makes it clear that what you are selling is not a Solution In Search Of A Problem (SISOAP).

Instead, an effective elevator pitch very explicitly explains the problem you are trying to solve, for whom it is a problem, and exactly why it is a problem.

4. CREDIBLE

An effective elevator pitch explains why you are qualified to see the problem and to build the solution.

While you may be supremely confident that the world needs the Solution you are selling, when it comes to persuading others to back you, faith alone isn't enough.

Instead, you must give people a reason to believe what you are saying.

As a result, an effective elevator pitch addresses the question of the credentials and qualifications of the team. The goal is to convince the audience that you know what you are talking about and that you have the knowledge, experience, and resources that are required to get the job done.

5. CONCEPTUAL

An effective elevator pitch stays at a fairly high level and does not go into too much unnecessary detail.

Too often, when writing, developing, and delivering their elevator pitches, people spend much too much time talking about HOW their Solution works and HOW they are going to bring it to life and not nearly enough time explaining WHAT their Solution is, WHO will buy it, and WHY they will buy it.

Why this happens is perfectly understandable. When it comes to bringing an idea to life, you have to spend an inordinate amount of time thinking about questions of HOW you will bring your Solution to life. However, when you are explaining your Solution to someone you have never spoken to before, you must first ensure that they know WHAT it is that you are talking about before you start to answer all of the HOW questions that you are preoccupied with.

6. CONCRETE

As much as is possible, an effective elevator pitch is also specific and tangible.

While it's important that an elevator pitch doesn't get into too many operational and other unnecessary details, it is still important to make clear to the audience that your Solution isn't just an idea. Instead, you want to make sure that the audience comes away with the sense that what you are talking about is real (or soon will be).

That means talking about specific products and not just technologies. That also means talking about demonstrable accomplishments, assuming – and hoping – you have some.

7. CONSISTENT

Every version of an effective elevator pitch conveys the same basic message.

Research reveals that people have to be exposed to a message three times before it will start to sink in. As a result, while you must have different versions of your elevator pitch, each of which is tailored to the interests of the audience with which you will speak, those different versions must be similar. That way, regardless of which version of your elevator pitch a person hears, they will still come to the same basic understanding of who you are and what it is that you are selling.

8. CUSTOMIZED

An effective elevator pitch addresses the specific interests and concerns of the audience.

The way to get someone's attention is to speak their language; to answer the questions they want to ask without their having to ask them. The way to do that is to customize your elevator pitch so that you can deliver (slightly) different versions to each of the different audiences with which you wish to speak.

In the case of a start-up company, this means having customized versions of your elevator pitch that target prospective team members, business partners, investors, and customers.

9. CONVERSATIONAL

An effective elevator pitch is designed to start a conversation with the audience.

As I said before, one reason why so many elevator pitches go into so much unnecessary detail, and end up being so ineffective, is that too few people understand the goal of an elevator pitch. Rather than being to close the deal, the goal of an elevator pitch is to just get the ball rolling. Generally, that means starting a conversation, or a dialogue, with the audience. Only during later conversations will the audience be interested in the details – the HOW – of your Solution.

3. SAMPLE ELEVATOR PITCHES

> *"It is with words as with sunbeams. The more they are condensed, the deeper they burn."*
> – Robert Southey

In my work with would-be entrepreneurs, I have found that one of the hardest parts of putting together an elevator pitch is that very few people know what an elevator pitch looks like, much less what an effective elevator pitch looks like.

With that in mind, let me give you a couple of examples of elevator pitches with which I am personally familiar and explain how, and why, they comply with The Nine C's.

- **SalesLogix**
- **Elevator Pitch Essentials**
- **Personal Elevator Pitch**

The SalesLogix elevator pitch was written to introduce potential investors, business partners, and customers to a new software company. The Elevator Pitch Essentials elevator pitch was written to sell this book to literary agents and publishers. The personal elevator pitch is one I use to sell myself to potential clients.

3.1. SALESLOGIX

> *"It is my ambition to say in ten sentences what other men say in whole books."*
> – Nietzsche

A number of years ago, I had the good fortune to join a start-up called SalesLogix that sold a middle market Customer Relationship Management (CRM) product. SalesLogix shipped its first product in 1997, went public in 1999, and was acquired in 2001 in a deal valued at $263 million. The early 1997 version of the SalesLogix elevator pitch – which we used to raise a total of $17 million – went like this...

> SalesLogix is a software company and has developed a Customer Relationship Management (CRM) system that is both easier to use and more powerful than existing solutions like Act and Siebel.
>
> The problem with existing CRM solutions is that they fall into one of two categories. On the one hand, you have contact managers like Act that salespeople love but that do not allow people to share information across a large organization. On the other hand you have high-end CRM systems like Siebel that scale to support the needs of hundreds or thousands of users but that salespeople refuse to use. The result is that too many organizations are unable to...
>
> • Coordinate their sales and customer service teams.
> • Obtain a holistic picture of the customer.
> • Maximize the revenue gained from each customer.
>
> In contrast, SalesLogix delivers the best of both worlds...
>
> • The affordability and ease of use of a contact manager.
> • The scalability, database synchronization, customization, and reporting capabilities of a high-end CRM system.

> SalesLogix is targeting midsized companies that have outgrown contact managers like Act but can't afford the cost and complexity of high-end CRM products like Siebel.
>
> The SalesLogix team has over 75 years of combined experience in the industry and is led by Pat Sullivan, the co-founder and former CEO of Contact Software International, the original developer of Act.
>
> SalesLogix is seeking $5 million to finance the continued development and marketing of SalesLogix 1.0, which is scheduled to be released in April 1997.

Now that you've seen the entire SalesLogix elevator pitch, let me explain the logic behind it in terms of The Nine C's.[1]

1. CONCISE

The entire SalesLogix elevator pitch contained 250 words and, as a result, could be comfortably delivered in just under two minutes...

> SalesLogix is a software company and has developed a Customer Relationship Management (CRM) system that is both easier to use and more powerful than existing solutions like Act and Siebel.

What's more, the key points of the SalesLogix elevator pitch were contained in the summary sentence (the first paragraph), which contained just 30 words.

2. CLEAR

One way we ensured that the SalesLogix elevator pitch was clear was by using only a single acronym (CRM), and by defining that acronym in the body of the elevator pitch.

A second way that we ensured that the SalesLogix elevator pitch was clear was by talking about our product in relation to products, like Act and Siebel, that the audience was likely to have already heard about. While what we were doing was new and different, we also knew that, when hearing our elevator pitch, people would compare us to what they already knew. As a result, our elevator pitch gave the audience two reference points that made clear our point of difference.

A third way that we ensured that the SalesLogix elevator pitch was clear was through the judicious use of repetition. Repetition can help people to remember a message. As a result, we essentially restated our summary sentence two thirds of the way through our elevator pitch...

SalesLogix is targeting mid-sized companies that have outgrown contact managers like Act but can't afford the cost and complexity of high-end CRM products like Siebel.

Finally, whenever we delivered our elevator pitch, we tried to accompany it with a positioning diagram that reiterated our sense of the problem and our point of difference. In fact, this diagram was so helpful that when we couldn't use a slide show or white board to get this point across, we would use our hands to paint this picture for the audience.

3. COMPELLING

Because of our experience in the industry, we knew that the problem with the state of the art was that existing CRM packages made companies feel like they had to make an impossible choice between usability and power…

The problem with existing CRM solutions is that they fall into one of two categories. On the one hand, you have contact managers like Act that salespeople love but that do not allow people to share information across a large organization. On the other hand you have high-end CRM systems like Siebel that scale to support the needs of hundreds or thousands of users but that sales-people refuse to use. The result is that too many organizations are unable to…

- *Coordinate their sales and customer service teams.*
- *Obtain a holistic picture of the customer.*
- *Maximize the revenue gained from each customer.*

As a result, our elevator pitch – as well as all of our marketing and other communication pieces – reiterated the theme that SalesLogix was both easy to use and powerful (with "both" being the critical word)…

In contrast, SalesLogix delivers the best of both worlds…

- *The affordability and ease of use of a contact manager.*
- *The scalability, database synchronization, customization, and reporting capabilities of a high-end CRM system.*

4. CREDIBLE

The key advantage that we had at SalesLogix was our credibility, and we used it to our advantage. We had done this before, and this gave customers, investors, business partners, and the press and analysts an extra reason to listen to what we had to say. As a result, our elevator pitch reminded the audience of our credentials...

> *The SalesLogix team has over 75 years of combined experience in the industry and is led by Pat Sullivan, the co-founder and former CEO of Contact Software International, the original developer of Act.*

We also used the same strategy in our advertising by prominently featuring Pat Sullivan's story and image in all of our advertising, sales, and marketing materials. Also, wherever possible – and regardless of whether we were talking to investors, analysts, or customers – our message was delivered by Pat Sullivan himself.

5. CONCEPTUAL

Rather than getting into technical details like HOW the database synchronization system worked or operational details like our intention to sell the product through a network of business partners, the SalesLogix elevator pitch instead stayed at a fairly high level and focused on first answering basic questions like...

- **What** is it? A Customer Relationship Management (CRM) system.
- **Who** needs it? Mid-sized organizations that need a system that is both easy to use and powerful.
- **Why** do they need it? Existing solutions did not satisfy the needs of organizations as they grow.
- **WhoRU** to see the problem and to create the solution? The SalesLogix team has over 75 years of combined experience and is led by industry veteran Pat Sullivan.

6. CONCRETE

While the SalesLogix elevator pitch was fairly conceptual in nature, it was still very concrete and specific when it came to...

- **The Customer** – Mid-sized organizations who have outgrown contact managers like Act but who cannot afford the cost and complexity of high-end CRM systems like Siebel.
- **The Problem** – Existing solutions are either easy to use or powerful, but not both.
- **The Competition** – Contact managers like Act and high-end CRM systems like Siebel.
- **The Team** – Led by Pat Sullivan and with over 75 years of combined experience in the industry.
- **The Objective** – Raise $5 million to finance the continued development and marketing of SalesLogix 1.0.

7. CONSISTENT

Regardless of the audience, every version of the SalesLogix elevator pitch communicated the same basic message; that SalesLogix offered the affordability and ease of use of contact managers and the power of high-end CRM systems. This basic message was then distilled down into a tagline that was consistent with and reinforced our core message and positioning. The initial version of the SalesLogix tagline was...

> *SalesLogix is the first Act-like CRM solution.*

Over time, our tagline evolved into something that was even clearer...

> *SalesLogix is the first true CRM solution that's as easy to use as Act.*

Both taglines only mentioned Act, and not Siebel as well, both for reasons of length and simplicity and because of Pat Sullivan's history as the creator of Act.

8. CUSTOMIZED

During early 1997, when this version of the SalesLogix elevator pitch was written, we were talking to multiple groups: venture capitalists, potential customers, analysts and the press, and business partners. As a result, we developed different versions to speak to these different groups. However, regardless of which audience we were speaking to, each version focused on the problem we were solving and our previous experience solving it.

9. CONVERSATIONAL

One reason we structured the SalesLogix pitch as we did was that we knew that some people knew a lot about the CRM market but most didn't know the market very well. As a result, we were able to able to tweak our delivery in mid-pitch depending on the signals we received from the audience. If it was clear that they were familiar with the market, we would go with a slightly lower-level version of the pitch. If we got the sense that the audience was unfamiliar with the market, then we would stick with the elevator pitch as it was written. However, in either case the audience would generally be interested in learning more about what we were doing.

3.2. ELEVATOR PITCH ESSENTIALS

"Good things, when short, are twice as good."
– Baltasar Gracian

As I was writing this book and talking about it with my friends and family, they would constantly ask me, "So what's your book about?" After having this happen to me 10 or so times, and stumbling through an answer to that question, I realized I needed to follow my own advice and come up with an elevator pitch for Elevator Pitch Essentials. After going through a number of iterations, I ended up with this ...

> Elevator Pitch Essentials *is a business book that explains to entrepreneurs, innovators, project champions, and others the secrets of writing and delivering an effective elevator pitch.*
>
> *When you are selling an idea for a new product, service, project, or other Solution, you frequently come across situations where you meet someone who can help you achieve your goal, but you do not have the time to give them a complete, detailed, formal presentation.*
>
> That includes situations like...
> • *Running into an executive in an elevator.*
> • *Meeting an influential person in a bar or buffet line.*
> • *Being introduced to a potential investor.*
> • *Introducing yourself to a group of people.*
>
> *...and being asked to explain who you are and what you are doing.*
> *Unless you want to come across as boorish and self-centered, you only have a few seconds – or in the best case a couple of minutes – to get your point across. As a result, you have to be prepared to give someone a quick overview of your Solution and leave the details to later.*

> Elevator Pitch Essentials *teaches people how to handle those kinds of situations.*
>
> Elevator Pitch Essentials *grew out of my experience writing elevator pitches for a series of startups I worked for or with. About 5 years ago, I pulled all that knowledge together and put together a seminar about elevator pitches for Washington University in St. Louis. I then turned that presentation into this book.*

As you can see, I followed the advice I give in this book when writing the elevator pitch for Elevator Pitch Essentials.

1. CONCISE

The *Elevator Pitch Essentials* summary sentence contains just 27 words and the entire elevator pitch contains just 244 words. As a result, the summary sentence can be delivered in less than 15 seconds and the entire pitch can be delivered in less than 2 minutes.

2. CLEAR

I start the *Elevator Pitch Essentials* elevator pitch with a relatively short summary sentence in order to ensure that it is clear...

> Elevator Pitch Essentials *is a business book that explains to entrepreneurs, innovators, project champions, and others the secrets of writing and delivering an effective elevator pitch.*

I did this because I wanted to make sure that the listener would have a sense of where I was going before I got too far into the details. The nice thing about this summary sentence was that it could stand on its own but also gave the listener a preview of my entire elevator pitch.

3. COMPELLING

After giving my summary sentence, I immediately launch into a discussion of the problem the book solves. In this case, I do it through the use of a number of scenarios that people can easily relate to...

> *When you are selling an idea for a new product, service, project, or other Solution, you frequently come across situations where you meet someone who can help you achieve your goal, but you do not have the time to give them a complete, detailed, formal presentation.*

That includes situations like...
- *Running into an executive in an elevator.*
- *Meeting an influential person in a bar or buffet line.*
- *Being introduced to a potential investor.*
- *Introducing yourself to a group of people.*

...and being asked to explain who you are and what you are doing.

Unless you want to come across as boorish and self-centered, you only have a few seconds – or in the best case a couple of minutes – to get your point across. As a result, you have to be prepared to give someone a quick overview of your Solution and leave the details to later.

Elevator Pitch Essentials teaches people how to handle those kinds of situations.

Explaining the problem that you solve through three or four scenarios is a good way of making sure that your elevator pitch is both clear and compelling.

4. CREDIBLE

When it comes to non-fiction books, most people want to know that the writer is an expert in the field. As a result, in order to establish my credibility with the audience, I budgeted 50 or so words to explain my experience with writing and delivering elevator pitches...

Elevator Pitch Essentials grew out of my experience writing elevator pitches for a series of start-ups I worked for or with. About 5 years ago, I pulled all that knowledge together and put together a seminar about elevator pitches for Washington University in St. Louis. I then turned that presentation into this book.

The goal was to increase the likelihood that the audience would see me as an expert in the subject and take seriously what I had to say.

5. CONCEPTUAL

Instead of getting into the low-level details of the book, like the number and contents of each chapter, in the *Elevator Pitch Essentials* elevator pitch I instead talk about the problem the book solves and the intended audience for the book. If I find that someone wants to know more about my book, then I can go into the details, but not until then.

6. CONCRETE

The way I made my elevator pitch concrete was by building it around a scenario to which most people could relate. Nearly everyone has experienced that moment when they come face to face with the person who can help them achieve their goal. The problem is that too often people don't know what to do.

7. CONSISTENT

While I would tailor parts of my pitch to the audience, I started off every version of my pitch with the same summary sentence and concluded every version with the same statement of my credentials.

8. CUSTOMIZED

When speaking with or writing to literary agents, I would add the phrase "non-fiction" to my summary sentence just to make it absolutely clear what type of book I was writing...

> Elevator Pitch Essentials *is a non-fiction, business book that explains to entrepreneurs, innovators, project champions, and others the secrets of writing and delivering an effective elevator pitch.*

I did this because, just as venture capitalists tend to specialize in certain markets, so too do literary agents (and publishers). There are non-fiction literary agents and fiction literary agents. Within those two broad groups, there are many other subdivisions. I knew that literary agents who deal primarily in works of fiction wouldn't be interested in my book, and I didn't want to waste their time.

9. CONVERSATIONAL

The point of the *Elevator Pitch Essentials* elevator pitch wasn't to close the deal then and there. Instead, it was to just get a conversation started with a potential literary agent or buyer of the book. As a result, I didn't finish with a high-pressure close. Instead, I finished in a way that made it easy for the audience to ask a follow-up question if they were interested. If they weren't interested in the topic – if they didn't have a need to know how to create an elevator pitch – then I didn't want to waste their time or mine.

3.3. PERSONAL ELEVATOR PITCH

> *"True eloquence consists in saying all that should be said, and that only."*
> – Francois Duc de la Rochefoucauld

Breakfast clubs and similar business networking organizations are becoming an increasingly popular tool for service providers and other salespeople. In many cases, a key part of the morning's program is for each person to give a 1-minute elevator pitch that explains who they are and why they are there. When I attend such an event, the elevator pitch that I use goes like this...

> My name is Chris O'Leary and I teach entrepreneurs, salespeople, project champions, and others how to communicate their ideas to investors, customers, senior executives, and co-workers.
>
> For the past five years, I have been holding workshops at Washington University, teaching entrepreneurs how to pitch ideas for new products and services to venture capitalists and angel investors. Over the past year I have turned that workshop into a book that is applicable to anyone who wants to know how to improve their ability to pitch an idea to someone.
>
> My book and workshop draw upon lessons I learned while working with a series of software startups in sales and marketing roles.
>
> I would love to discuss my work with anyone who is interested after we are done.

Let me explain the logic of my personal elevator pitch in the context of The Nine C's.

1. CONCISE

Since my personal elevator pitch contains just 126 words, I can easily deliver it in one minute or less without sounding rushed.

2. CLEAR

In order to make sure that my personal elevator pitch is clear, I start it off with a summary sentence that explains what I do at a high level. The goal is to give people a general sense of who I am and what I do so that they can better understand what I say next. I am also trying to quickly catch the attention of potential clients and ensure that they will listen to my entire pitch.

3. COMPELLING

I am fairly subtle when it comes to making my personal elevator pitch compelling, because I know that many people understand the need to be a good communicator...

> *My name is Chris O'Leary and I teach entrepreneurs, salespeople, project champions, and others how to communicate their ideas to investors, customers, senior executives, and co-workers.*

My summary sentence lays out some of the common scenarios that I help people handle.

4. CREDIBLE

The middle of my elevator pitch is where I establish my credibility, and I do that in two ways. First, I explain my association with Washington University, which is a highly respected name in the field of education...

> *For the past five years, I have been holding workshops at Washington University, teaching entrepreneurs how to pitch ideas for new products and services to venture capitalists and angel investors.*

I then quickly discuss my personal experience with writing and delivering elevator pitches...

> *My book and workshop draw upon lessons I learned while working with a series of software startups in sales and marketing roles.*

The goal is to establish myself as a respected expert in the subject.

5. CONCEPTUAL

In my personal elevator pitch, I don't get into the HOW of my approach and methodology. Instead, I focus on establishing WHAT I do and why I am qualified to advise people on that topic.

6. CONCRETE

I establish the concreteness of what I am doing with the line below...

> *Over the past year I have turned that workshop into a book that is applicable to anyone who wants to know how to improve their ability to pitch an idea to someone.*

The goal is to let people know that I have two specific products that I sell: a book and a workshop.

7. CONSISTENT

My summary sentence lays out the different types of clients that I work with...

> *My name is Chris O'Leary and I teach entrepreneurs, salespeople, project champions, and others how to communicate their ideas to investors, customers, senior executives, and co-workers.*

As a result, I am able to deliver the same basic personal elevator pitch to a variety of different audiences and know it will appeal to a variety of different people.

8. CUSTOMIZED

If I am not sure who will be in the audience, or if the audience is mixed, then I deliver the basic version of my personal elevator pitch. However, if I am delivering my personal elevator pitch to a specific group, such as salespeople, then I will modify it so that it focuses on the needs of salespeople. I do that by modifying the last line of my personal elevator pitch so that it more directly speaks to the needs of salespeople...

> *I would love to discuss my work with you in detail afterwards and explain how I can help you close more deals.*

9. CONVERSATIONAL

In order to ensure that my personal elevator pitch is conversational, I close with an invitation to discuss my work afterwards...

> *I would love to discuss my work with anyone who is interested after we are done.*

I keep my close low pressure and soft sell because in my experience I have found that people aren't ready to buy immediately after hearing my personal elevator pitch. Instead, they want to know more about how I can help them with their specific situation.

4. THE NINE C'S

> *"He who talks more is sooner exhausted."*
> – Lao Tzu

Now that I've given you an overview of what an elevator pitch is, let me drop down a level and get into some of the details of an effective elevator pitch. I will do this by going into detail about The Nine C's of an effective elevator pitch...

1. **Concise**
2. **Clear**
3. **Compelling**
4. **Credible**
5. **Conceptual**
6. **Concrete**
7. **Consistent**
8. **Customized**
9. **Conversational**

When thinking about The Nine C's, it's important to keep in mind that they don't just apply to the elevator pitch. Rather, they represent the keys to effective communication in a wide variety of settings.

4.1. CONCISE

> *"I didn't have the time to write a short letter, so I wrote a long one instead."*
> – Mark Twain

Back in the dot-com days, a friend and I shopped around an idea for a startup. One of the people we talked to was my friend's brother-in-law, a man named Doug. Doug managed the money of wealthy families, and because wealthy people often do a lot of angel investing, we knew that getting Doug interested in our idea could really help our cause.

As we walked into Doug's office, he was on the phone, checking his e-mail, and talking to his secretary at the same time. We asked him if he was ready for us and he said "Yes" so we started to give him our pitch. He listened to us for about 5 minutes and then got up to do something at his desk. We asked him if he wanted us to pause, but he told us to keep going. This went on for another 25 minutes or so, with Doug doing three different things during the pitch. While we were a little thrown by this, at the end of the 30 minutes Doug told us that he was interested in our idea and that he wanted us to speak to some guys that he knew. That meeting led to a series of others that help us move our idea forward.

While a bit disconcerting at the time, I have come to learn that our experience with Doug wasn't that unusual. Powerful people tend to be extremely busy. Each year a venture capitalist will talk to thousands of people and review hundreds of business plans. Similarly, senior executives are constantly being asked to decide what is a priority and what to invest their budgets in.

That means their time is precious.

As a result, the way to get their attention, and to impress them, is to be able to quickly get to the point; to be able to explain what you need, and why, in just a few seconds or at most minutes.

THE ACCORDION MODEL

Before you get the idea that what I'm saying is that your elevator pitch should simply be short, keep in mind that you don't want to waste any of the time that you have been given. While in some cases you may only have ten or twenty seconds to deliver your pitch, in other cases you may have as much as two minutes.

As a result, a good way to think of your elevator pitch is like an accordion.[2]

If you keep your hands close together, then an accordion is narrow and compact. If you spread your hands apart, then an accordion is wide and expansive.

An effective elevator pitch must be able to do the same thing; it must be able to be short and focused if necessary, but must also be able to expand and fill the time that is available.

If you are asked to introduce yourself to a group of people, then you must be able to get your point across in just 10 or 15 seconds. However, if you meet someone while standing in a bar line at a wedding or other social function, you may have as much as a minute or two.

WORD LIMITS

When you are writing your elevator pitch, the first thing to keep in mind is that most people can comfortably speak at around 125 words per minute. As a result, when it comes to a word budget for your elevator pitch, you're talking about 25 or so words on the low side and 250 words at the absolute maximum.

If in doubt, you should stay under the 250-word limit because it is much better to speak slowly and in a calm and relaxed manner than it is to be rushed. By rushing through your elevator pitch, you are more likely to damage your credibility by sounding harried and disorganized than you are to help yourself by getting in that one extra sentence.

THE INVERTED PYRAMID

When writing an elevator pitch, I am always deliberately a little paranoid and assume that the speaker will be cut off at any moment. As a result, I try to follow the inverted pyramid model that is used by newspapers.

The inverted pyramid model says that, rather than burying the most important information in the body of a story, you should instead start the story with it. That way, someone can get the gist of the story by reading just the first line or two of the story (which is called the "Lede"). They can then keep on reading if they want more information or details.

In the case of a newspaper, the most important information – and the key contents of the Lede – are the Who, What, Where, When, and Why of the story.

THE SUMMARY SENTENCE

In the case of an elevator pitch, the equivalent of the Lede is something that I call the summary sentence. In the same way that your elevator pitch is a summary of your Solution, your summary sentence is a summary of your elevator pitch. As a result, your summary sentence is the most critical element of your elevator pitch; it is what you should say if you only have time to say one thing.

The job of the summary sentence is to provide the audience with a quick, crisp overview of what you are doing. By quick, I mean no longer than 25 words and able to be delivered in just 10 or so seconds. By crisp, I mean something that is well-organized and that flows off the tongue easily. By overview, I mean something that focuses on the WHAT of your idea and that leaves the HOW to a later conversation.

There are three reasons why it is important to start off your elevator pitch with a summary sentence.

First, and most importantly, people start forming an impression of others in just a few seconds and, as the old adage says, you never get a second chance to make a first impression. You want people's first impression of you to be of someone who is organized and articulate, not someone who is disorganized and long-winded.

Second, when encountering any new piece of information, people quickly decide whether to pay attention to it or not; whether what they are seeing, reading, or hearing is relevant or not. You want the answer to that question to be "Yes."

Third, in most cases you have no way of knowing in advance just how much time you have to talk to a person; it may be 10 seconds or it may be 10 minutes. It is safest to be paranoid and assume that you only have a short period of time. If it turns out that you have more time, then you can always go into more detail.

WHAT TO INCLUDE

An effective summary sentence focuses on several things.

Company Name – Just as you should tell someone your name when introducing yourself, your summary sentence should give the name of your company, team, or project. That name will give them a piece of information off of which they can hang all of the other information you are going to provide.

Type of Company – Investors do not invest in any and every type of venture. Instead, they tend to specialize in just a few sectors and types of products. As a result, one way to make it clear that you know what you are doing is to help professional investors decide whether to pay attention to you or not by indicating the type of company you are (e.g. a hardware or software company) in your summary sentence. If they don't cover your type of Solution, they aren't going to back you anyway, so its best to not waste their time. In addition, when talking about what type of company you are in your summary sentence, it isn't necessary to mention the stage of the company. This is a level of detail that is best left to later on in your elevator pitch (e.g. the objective).

Category – In a similar vein, your summary sentence should establish what category (e.g. life sciences or customer relationship management) your Solution is targeting.

Product or Service Name – One way to make your venture feel more tangible is to tell the audience the name of your product or service. That communicates that you are selling more than just an idea.

Key Benefit(s) – If you want to give the audience a high-level sense that you understand selling, your summary sentence must answer the "So what?" question. It must identify the one or two things that differentiate your idea from existing solutions and that will drive people to change.

One place to look for benefits is to look to your answer to the question, "What's wrong with the state of the art?" Your key benefits should be the opposite of what's wrong with the state of the art.

Chief Competitor(s) – In some cases, naming you chief competitor(s) can help people understand what you are doing.

EXAMPLES

Since the summary sentence is the most important part of an elevator pitch, and in many cases will determine the success of your entire elevator pitch, let me give you some examples of what a good summary sentence looks like.

SalesLogix – The SalesLogix summary sentence touched on each of the elements I mention above...

> *SalesLogix is a software company and has developed a Customer Relationship Management (CRM) system that is both easier to use and more powerful than existing solutions like Act and Siebel.*

Since we knew that hardware venture capitalists wouldn't be interested in our deal and we didn't want to waste their time or ours, the SalesLogix summary sentence made it clear that we were a software company and not a hardware or services company. The SalesLogix elevator pitch named the market segment we were targeting – the Customer Relationship Management market – and used the full name of the category before giving the acronym in case some people had heard the acronym before but didn't know what it meant. The SalesLogix elevator pitch also listed our two key benefits, rather than just our two key features. Finally, the SalesLogix elevator pitch named our two reference competitors because this helped people understand how we fit into the market and our point of difference.

Elevator Pitch Essentials – The *Elevator Pitch Essentials* summary sentence followed a slightly different format because, while SalesLogix was trying to carve out a piece of an existing market, *Elevator Pitch Essentials* was targeting relatively virgin terrain. There were no direct competitors, and few indirect competitors, for *Elevator Pitch Essentials*, which is why the opportunity existed in the first place...

> *Elevator Pitch Essentials is a business book that explains to entrepreneurs, innovators, project champions, and others the secrets of writing and delivering an effective elevator pitch.*

The *Elevator Pitch Essentials* summary sentence explained that the book was a business book because I knew that, like venture capitalists, literary agents and publishers tend to be specialists. Not every literary agent and publisher would be interested in my book because they might work with fiction or other titles. As a result, I put that phrase up front in my summary sentence so that the audience could quickly and easily decide whether to pay attention to my pitch or not. I also used the phrase "entrepreneurs, innovators, project champions, and others" in order to explain to the audience that the book would appeal to more than just entrepreneurs, who are the traditional users of elevator pitches.

SUMMARY SENTENCES VERSUS TAGLINES

Keep in mind that a summary sentence is different than a tagline. A tagline is even shorter than a summary sentence because it is generally limited to the benefits of the Solution. However, a tagline does not contain enough detail to serve as a summary sentence.

SPLITTING HAIRS

Before I close this chapter, let me explain that if, during the course of putting together your elevator pitch, you find yourself arguing over individual words you should understand that this is perfectly normal. I remember that back in the days when I was working for SalesLogix, I would get very frustrated with my boss due to just two words that we used in our elevator pitch. He thought we should describe the customer and the problem as follows...

> SalesLogix is targeting mid-sized companies that have outgrown contact managers like Act but <u>don't need</u> the cost and complexity of high-end CRM products like Siebel.

I thought that sentence was almost perfect, but the phrase "don't need" was a little weak. I preferred the version below because of the strong, double meaning of the phrase "can't afford"...

> SalesLogix is targeting mid-sized companies that have outgrown contact managers like Act but <u>can't afford</u> the cost and complexity of high-end CRM products like Siebel.

While it may seem like I was just splitting hairs, and that there was little real difference between the two versions, this disagreement reflects how hard it can be to create an effective elevator pitch. Given the word limits that are necessary for an elevator pitch or summary sentence, you have to choose each word very carefully. That's one reason why it can often be harder to write something short than to write something long.

YOUR SUMMARY SENTENCE

I have found that effective elevator pitches generally start off with a summary sentence, which is a short overview of your Solution that, if necessary, can stand alone. Below is a good format for a summary sentence...

> *COMPANY NAME is a TYPE OF COMPANY and has developed a PRODUCT CATEGORY that is KEY BENEFIT(S) than existing solutions (like CHIEF COMPETITORS).*

The SalesLogix elevator pitch fits into this format...

> *SalesLogix is a software company and has developed a Customer Relationship Management (CRM) system that is both more powerful and easier to use than existing solutions like Act and Siebel.*

Take a few minutes and try to fit your Solution into this template and see how it flows. Keep in mind that your goal is to end up with a summary sentence that is approximately 25 words or less.

4.2. CLEAR

> *"Clarity is so obviously one of the attributes of the truth that very often it passes for truth."*
>
> – Joseph Joubert

One of my most vivid memories from my childhood goes back to a trip I took when I was 12 or so. My parents, my two younger brothers, and I went to Kentucky Lake for a family reunion, and one of the activities was a day of water-skiing with my older cousins, who ranged in age from 15 to 22.

We showed up at 11AM or so, after they had been water-skiing for a couple of hours. They brought the boat in to shore, picked us up, and then went back out a couple hundred feet or so. Being the oldest, I said I was going first, so I put on a life jacket, jumped in the water, and slipped my feet into the two water skis.

I don't remember what I was thinking as the boat moved away from me and they started to take the slack out of the line. However, what happened next is burned in my brain.

I gave the boat a thumbs up to indicate that I was ready and I braced myself the best I could for whatever was going to happen next. At that point, my cousin who was driving the boat hit it. However, he apparently forgot that he had a 75-pound, 12-year-old newbie water-skier at the end of the line and not a 200+ pound, 22 year-old, expert water-skier. What I remember is being instantly jerked out of the water, flying up and over the ends of my skis, landing face-first in the murky green water, and being pulled out of my skis and under the water until I had the good sense to let go of the towrope.

So what does this have to do with an elevator pitch?

The problem is that too many would-be entrepreneurs – and in particular engineers, scientists, and other technologists – do the same basic thing to the audience. Instead of easing the audience into a discussion of their Solution, they hit it. They launch into a low-level, lingo-laden explanation of their Solution without taking into account the experience, or interests, of the audience. More often than not, this causes the audience to simply tune out both the pitch and the pitcher.

THE MINDSET OF EFFECTIVE COMMUNICATORS

In the water-skiing story, it wasn't my fault that I flopped over onto my face. I had never water-skied before, and the driver of the boat should have taken my skills and abilities into account. As a result, at the end of the day the fault for my problems learning how to water ski lies primarily with the driver of the boat.

When it comes to communicating one's message, the same principle applies. When communicating a message to an audience, it is the job of the communicator, not the audience, to make sure the message is understood.

The logic behind this principle is that because the communicator possesses all of the information, it is their job to figure out how to communicate it in an effective manner. There is only so much the audience can contribute, other than making sure that they are paying attention.

Effective communicators understand this critical principle and take responsibility for ensuring that they are understood. Unfortunately, too many would-be communicators engage in "blame the victim" thinking and refuse to take responsibility for problems they create for the audience.

I once worked for a company that was having problems with a certain part of its web site. The issue was that the users of the system were having a hard time figuring out how to use it. I knew these problems were costing us revenue, so I jumped into the middle of the issue to try to see if I could come up with a solution. I quickly came to understand that a root cause of the problem was the attitudes of the people in charge of the system. In conversations with them about the problems that users were having, they told me things like, "We can't help it if they're too stupid to understand what they need to do." and, more generally, "You can't fix stupid."

The truth was that things were never going to get better, and revenues were never going to reach their potential, until the people who had the power to fix the problem took responsibility for their actions and started to take seriously their role as communicators.

EXPERTS AND ORDINARY PEOPLE

If you want to become an effective communicator, you first need to understand that the world is made up of two very different types of people: Experts and Ordinary People.[3] Among other things – some of which I will discuss in the next chapter – these two types of people have very different levels of knowledge about, and interest in, a given subject.

Experts – Experts make up 10 percent or so of the population and tend to be the innovative types of the world. They are the people who know more about a given subject than nearly anyone. They are so much more knowledgeable about that subject because they are more interested in it than nearly anyone else. Most entrepreneurs tend to be Experts, at least when it comes to their Solution.

Ordinary People – Ordinary People make up the other 90 percent of the world and are just that. They are regular folks who know a lot about a lot of things, but not as much as the Experts of the world. In general, Ordinary People know just enough to get by, but really aren't interested in learning more about a given Solution than they need to.

One thing that distinguishes effective communicators from unsuccessful ones is that they understand this difference. They understand that they are an Expert and that most people aren't like them; that most people don't share their level of knowledge about, or interest in, their Solution. As a result, they spend a tremendous amount of time and effort figuring out the best way to get their message across to Ordinary People.

HOW TO BE CLEAR

When listening to your pitch, potential investors, backers, and partners aren't just judging your technical and operational skills.

They are also judging your skills as a communicator.

They want to know that you understand the importance of constructing a message that will appeal to Ordinary People and not just Experts. They know that there is no point in backing someone who will not be able to raise additional money or sell their product to Ordinary People.

As a result, your elevator pitch must convince the audience that you understand how, and how important it is, to be clear. As I discussed in the previous chapter, one good way to do that is to start your elevator pitch off with a summary sentence. However, there are a number of other things that you have to do to ensure that you are clear.

Speak English – One way to ensure that you are being clear is by speaking English.

First, speaking English means not using any big, multi-syllabic words or words that someone may have to look up in a dictionary. Not only might using big words leave people confused, it can leave them feeling a little paranoid. Con men frequently try to put things over on people by using big words and unfamiliar phrases in the hope that the audience will trust them and think that they are smarter than they really are.

Second, speaking English means not using any acronyms. Every field of work develops its own acronyms and abbreviations. While these serve to make life easier for the people in that field, they also serve to exclude people. When selling your Solution, you want to make sure that the audience knows that you understand how to get your message out to the widest possible audience, not just the few people who are members of the club.

Oversimplify Things – One objection I frequently hear when coaching people with technical backgrounds is that they don't want to oversimplify things; that they are afraid to "dumb down" their Solution. While I understand the driving force behind this objection – in some cultures the way to impress people is to use big words – to create an effective elevator pitch you absolutely must "dumb down" your message. There simply isn't time to get into the technical nitty gritty of your Solution in just a minute or two. Instead, all you can hope to do is give people a general sense of what you are doing and why.

Tie Together Features and Benefits – A common characteristic of poor elevator pitches is that they contain long lists of features but do not explain the corresponding benefits. All this does is overwhelm people with disconnected, disjointed pieces of information that do not seem to fit together. As a result, none of this information is remembered and the audience is left more, rather than less, confused.

A better way to explain what's so special about your Solution is to list just a few (e.g. no more than two or three) key features and to give a one-sentence description of the benefits that each feature provides. In other words, after listing each feature, immediately answer the "So what?" question that the audience will naturally ask.

Use the Problem > Solution > Benefit Structure – A related approach that often significantly improves the clarity of an elevator pitch is to follow the Problem > Solution > Benefit structure. When explaining your Solution, first explain the problem that is being caused by the state of the art. Then explain what the solution looks like (at a very high level). Then explain the benefit that the customer will realize from your Solution.

Leverage the Known – An industry with significant experience pitching ideas to busy executives is Hollywood. Every year, hundreds of movies are released to theatres. Of course, before any movie can be released, it must first be made. That means that the person with the idea – usually the producer, writer, or director – has to convince the person with the money – usually a studio executive – to give them the money they need to turn their dream into a reality.

Sound familiar?

As it turns out, one technique that is widely used in Hollywood pitch meetings can help you explain your Solution to an audience of Ordinary People. The best way to see this technique in action is to rent Robert Altman's movie *The Player*.

Scattered throughout this movie are a number of scenes in which people pitch movies using the X meets Y template.

As *Ghost* meets *The Manchurian Candidate*, *Out of Africa* meets *Pretty Woman*, and *The Gods Must be Crazy* but with a TV actress instead of a Coke bottle.

I often use this technique to quickly communicate the concept of movies I like to my friends and relatives. For example, in telling my friends about the movie *Cloverfield*, I described it as a cross between *Godzilla* and *The Blair Witch Project*. That got across the idea that it's a monster movie filmed from a first-person perspective.

Why does this technique work?

First, it works because it explains new ideas in terms of two things the audience already knows. As much as you believe that your idea is new and unique, people will still want to know, "What's it like?" and "How's it different?" Rather then getting annoyed, you should use this tendency to want to relate the unknown to the known to your advantage.

Second, this technique works because it explains the new idea in terms of two things that were already successful. Experienced Hollywood pitch masters don't pitch movies as *Gigli* meets *Battlefield Earth* (a truly frightening thought). Instead, it is *Titanic* meets *E.T.*, *Gladiator* meets *Star Wars*, and *Shrek* meets *Tootsie* (or whatever).

Use Metaphors and Analogies – Using metaphors or analogies can help make your Solution clear. When selling SalesLogix, we would often describe SalesLogix as being "Act on Steroids" or "Like Act but for large sales forces." This helped to get our basic point across and gave people a sense of what we were doing and why.

Use a Prop – I once heard a pitch for a gas spectrometer start-up that had significantly shrunk the size of the device. The pitch wasn't that compelling when I first heard it, but after their pitch I started talking to them and it came out that they had reduced a mass spectrometer from the size of a washing machine to the size of a quarter. I thought that was a very significant difference, and I told the presenter that he should always have quarter with him so that he could show it to the audience at the appropriate time.

Props can also be useful tools for companies that have already developed a prototype of their product. Not only does it help people understand exactly what you are talking about, it can also help you look more concrete.

Repeat Yourself – One of the basic principles of effective communication is that repetition enhances clarity. Advertisers have found that most Ordinary People have to hear something 3 times in order to be able recall it reliably. That is why they run the same commercial over and over again. That is also why the first rule of effective presentations is to tell people what you are going to tell them, tell them, and then tell them what you told them. An effective elevator pitch follows the same basic format. The Summary Sentence tells them what you are going to tell them, the body of your elevator pitch tells them, and your close tells them what you told them.

Use Progressive Revelation – A final way of improving the clarity of an elevator pitch is to use an approach that I call "progressive revelation." This is a fancy way of saying that you should repeat yourself, but each time you do so you should give the audience just a little more information and detail. This is basically what is achieved by starting a pitch off with a summary sentence and then following it up with additional body text. The body text says the same basic thing as the summary sentence, but at a slightly lower level of detail. The point is to absolutely hammer home the one key message of the pitch, rather than trying to make multiple points in the pitch (which is generally less effective).

THE EXAMPLE OF SALESLOGIX

Let me go through the SalesLogix elevator pitch and explain some elements that helped make it more clear...

> *SalesLogix is a software company and has developed a Customer Relationship Management (CRM) system that is both easier to use and more powerful than existing solutions like Act and Siebel.*
>
> *SalesLogix is targeting mid-sized companies that have outgrown contact managers like Act but can't afford the cost and complexity of high-end CRM products like Siebel.*
>
> *The problem with existing CRM solutions is that they fall into*

one of two categories. On the one hand, you have contact managers like Act that salespeople love but that do not allow people to share information across a large organization. On the other hand you have high-end CRM systems like Siebel that scale to support the needs of hundreds or thousands of users but that sales-people refuse to use.

First, while the SalesLogix elevator pitch contained an acronym, it was defined immediately after it was used. Second, the SalesLogix elevator pitch was fairly, and deliberately, redundant. Notice that the first two sentences say pretty much the same thing. However, the difference is that the second sentence focused more on the problem and the pain, rather than the benefits, and used the phrase "mid-sized companies" to emphasize that, while SalesLogix could be used by any company, we were initially targeting mid-sized companies. Finally, you can see some progressive revelation at work in the SalesLogix elevator pitch. Notice how the second sentence basically restates the first, but is a little more detailed and focused. Similarly, the third paragraph says the same basic things as the first two paragraphs, but gets into more detail.

HOW TO TELL IF YOU ARE BEING CLEAR

It is impossible for an expert in a subject to tell if their pitch is clear just by reading it. As a result, here are a few things you can do that will give you an objective sense of the clarity of your message.

Monitor Your Readability Scores – One way to judge whether you are succeeding in speaking English is to take advantage of the readability score that Microsoft Word calculates when you check the spelling and grammar of a document. Microsoft Word calculates this readability score by looking at the syllables per word and words per sentence in your document.

Try Your Message Out on Ordinary People – Your goal should be to create a pitch that is understandable by Ordinary People. The way to see if you've done that is to deliver your elevator pitch to your spouse, your grandparents, and even your children. If they are able to understand what you are talking about, then you are probably doing your job. If not, then you need to go back and reevaluate what you say and how you say it.

Have the Audience Deliver Your Elevator Pitch Right Back to You – One way of telling if you're being clear is to give your pitch to someone and to have them deliver your pitch right back to you. That serves two purposes. First, by having someone deliver your pitch right back to you, you can see what they keyed in on and change what you emphasize if necessary. Second, your goal should be to turn your audience into your salesforce; to spread your message via low-cost, high-credibility word of mouth advertising. By having the audience deliver your pitch back to you, you can see how they will spread your message for you. You can then make adjustments to your pitch if necessary so that the right message is spread.

Listen to the Audience's First Question – At one start-up I worked for, when pitching the company to investors the CEO would deliver a half-hour to hour-long presentation that he had honed over the course of a couple of years. What struck me was that invariably the first question the audience would ask after that time was up was, "So what exactly is it that you are doing?" After that happened a few times, and taking the question at face value, I came to realize that one reason we were having trouble getting traction was that Ordinary People had no idea what we were talking about. That version of our pitch was going right over their heads and needed to be completely restructured. Since then, when delivering a pitch I have learned to pay close attention to the first question the audience asks and use it to judge whether my pitch is effective or not.

4.3. COMPELLING

"People who go around trying to invent something fall on their tails. The best inventions come from people who are deeply involved in trying to solve a problem."
– Howard Head

In the world today there is this idea going around, popularized by books like *The Secret*, that people should never talk about problems and the pain they cause. Instead, they should be positive and only talk about opportunities. The promise is that by focusing on the positive, only good things will happen. Conversely, we are warned that by focusing on – or even thinking about – problems, pain, and other "negative" things, only bad things will come to pass. While that idea is of dubious merit in general, it is simply wrong when it comes to entrepreneurship and innovation.

There is no better way to make people happy than by solving a problem that is causing them significant physical or psychic pain.

If you study the lives and stories of successful entrepreneurs, intrapraneurs, and innovators, you will find that most are unabashed – and often serial – problem-solvers. They make their fortunes by finding, and then solving, good problems.

This principle is understood by experienced venture capitalists, angel investors, executives, and salespeople. As a result, they are constantly on the lookout for people who understand the importance of finding, and then solving, good problems.

THE CHALLENGE OF CHANGE

Why is solving a problem so important?

Solving a problem is important because of the well-established fact that most people do not like to change.[4]

They live in the same houses. They go to the same restaurants. They listen to the same music.

Even when things get bad, they still resist changing.

They remain in dysfunctional personal relationships. They stay friends with people who drive them crazy. They linger on in jobs they hate.

As a result, change is ultimately the thing that makes or breaks innovations.

If the customer changes and adopts your Solution, then you will be successful and If they don't, then you won't.

It's that simple.

The reason that solving a problem is so important to the success of your Solution is that the existence of a problem can increase the likelihood that the customer will change. It can provide the customer with the incentive to change and try something new.

But not always.

THE PARADOX OF PAIN

Unfortunately, as many entrepreneurs have learned, solving a problem is not enough to guarantee that people will change and adopt your Solution.

Thomas Jefferson discussed this phenomenon back in 1776 in The Declaration Of Independence...

> All experience hath shown that mankind are more disposed to suffer, while evils are sufferable, than to right themselves by abolishing the forms to which they are accustomed.

In other words, as long as things aren't too bad, people are generally more inclined to just put up with them than they are to change and do something about them. Only the presence of significant amounts of physical or psychic pain will consistently drive people to change and adopt your Solution.[5]

When, at the beginning of this chapter, I said that experienced venture capitalists, angel investors, executives, and salespeople are constantly on the lookout for good problems, I was talking about pain. A good problem is a problem that is causing the customer significant amounts of physical or psychic pain and is giving them plenty of incentive to change as a result. In contrast, an ordinary problem is a problem that results in things being less than ideal, but generally not bad enough to give the customer enough incentive to change.

If you are going to improve your odds of being successful, it is critically important that you understand the difference between good problems and ordinary problems.

THE 10X RULE

While they don't always talk about problems and pain, experienced venture capitalists clearly understand the relationship between pain, change, and innovation. For example, many venture capitalists talk about the 10X rule, which says that a Solution has to be 10 times better than the state of the art for it to have a reasonable chance of being successful. That means that it has to be 10 times faster, 1/10th the cost, or 1/10th the size. The logic behind the 10X rule is that only if your Solution represents an order of magnitude, or 10X, improvement over the state of the art will the customer be able to make a business case for, and justify, abandoning the state of the art and switching to your Solution.

WHAT'S WRONG WITH THE STATE OF THE ART?

One way to explain the problem you are trying to solve, and establish that it is causing the customer significant amounts of pain, is to answer the question, "What's wrong with the state of the art?" In the case of SalesLogix, the thing that was wrong with the state of the art – and that turned a mere problem into a real opportunity – was something called database synchronization. Existing CRM systems couldn't ensure that the database of every person in a large organization contained the same information as everyone else's. This caused numerous headaches for organizations and gave them a reason to consider purchasing SalesLogix. In fact, this problem was causing some organizations so much pain that they committed to buying SalesLogix long before it was finished.

In the SalesLogix elevator pitch, we spent a significant amount of time talking about both the problem and why we were qualified to solve it (e.g. our credentials). One way we did this was by naming our chief competitors and then explaining their limitations...

> On the one hand, you have contact managers like Act that salespeople love but that do not allow people to share information across a large organization. On the other hand, you have high-end CRM systems like Siebel that scale to support the needs of hundreds or thousands of users but that salespeople refuse to use.

This was an extremely successful approach because it helped to establish not just who we were, but did so using products with which the audience was already familiar.

WHAT IF THERE IS NO STATE OF THE ART?

Sometimes, explaining what's wrong with the state of the art doesn't work because there is no state of the art; there is no existing solution to the problem you are trying to solve. In that case, one way to structure an elevator pitch is around a short scenario. This is the approach I took when developing an elevator pitch for this book, which is really the first of its kind. In the elevator pitch for *Elevator Pitch Essentials*, I first lay out a common, and relevant situation...

> When you are selling an idea for a new product, service, project, or other Solution, you frequently meet people who can help you achieve your goal, but do not have the time to give them a complete, detailed presentation. That includes situations like...
>
> • Running into an executive in an elevator.
> • Meeting an influential person in a bar line.
> • Being introduced to a potential investor.
> • Introducing yourself to a group of people.

I then explain the challenge that such a situation presents...

> Unless you want to come across as boorish and self-centered, you only have a few seconds – or in the best case a couple of minutes – to get your point across. As a result, you have to be prepared to give someone a quick overview of your Solution and leave the details to later.

I then explain the problem that people are faced with...

> The problem is that too few people are prepared to handle those kinds of situations. As a result, they let opportunity walk out the door.

I then set up *Elevator Pitch Essentials* as the solution to that problem...

> *Elevator Pitch Essentials* teaches people how to handle those kinds of situations.

While it is usually better to name the state of the art if it exists, in many cases that simply isn't possible. In that case, the best approach to structuring your elevator pitch is to do what I did in the *Elevator Pitch Essentials* elevator pitch and use a short scenario that people can relate to and that clearly explains the nature of the problem.

4.4. CREDIBLE

> *"All credibility, all good conscience, all evidence of truth come only from the senses."*
> – Friedrich Nietzsche

When I started out working for start-ups and delivered elevator pitches to different audiences, I hardly considered the subject of credibility. I thought the superiority of our Solution would be self-evident and would be enough to convince people to believe what I had to say.

However, when I started working with the folks at Washington University in St. Louis and moved to the other side of the table – and started listening to, judging, and making investment decisions based on pitches rather than just giving them – I quickly came to understand why credibility is so important.

The problem is that when you listen to enough pitches, you quickly realize that a lot of them sound pretty good on the surface. Yes, some obviously make no sense, but many sound plausible.

However, the statistics will tell you that can't possibly be the case. Something like 75 to 90 percent of new products end up as failures. That is because most new products end up having some hidden, but fatal, flaw.

As a result, most professional investors and senior executives have learned to be paranoid when it comes to judging pitches. They are always on the lookout for the fatal flaw that will end up tanking what, on the surface, seems like a promising idea.

Experienced investors and executives have learned that one way to reduce the likelihood that an idea has a fatal flaw is to pay close attention to the credibility of the team. They have learned that if they put their money behind people who understand how the world really works – who understand how hard it really is to build and sell new products – then they will significantly increase the likelihood that their investments will pay off.

THE BIG QUESTIONS

When writing your elevator pitch, it is essential that you address the issue of credibility if you want to achieve your goals. In general, that means answering two questions.

What are Your Qualifications to See the Problem? – In your elevator pitch, you must explain what it is that enables you to see an opportunity that others have not been able to see.

Generally, the way to do that is by pointing out your extensive, personal knowledge of a particular market or customer. That is the thing that will give you a legitimate insight into the dynamics of the market and will give you a sense of the strengths and weaknesses of the various competitors.

The best way to establish your qualifications is by pointing out your direct experience with the market. The second best – by a long shot – way of doing that is via marketing research.

What are Your Qualifications to Build the Solution? – In your elevator pitch, you must also explain why you will be able to solve the problem that you see.

Many problems are very obvious to anyone who looks for them, but persist because nobody has figured out a way to solve them. If your pitch is to be effective, then you must explain why you possess the technical and other abilities that will enable you to solve a problem that nobody else has been able to solve.

CREDIBILITY BREAKERS

When you are explaining your qualifications to see the problem and to build the solution, there are certain things you must avoid because they can suggest that your Solution has an underlying fatal flaw.

Eating an Elephant – One thing that always makes me nervous – and that makes people look naïve – is when a couple of people who have virtually no money at the present moment explain that they are going to directly attack a multi-billion dollar company or market. The problem isn't the ambition; the best ideas often have gigantic implications. Instead, the problem is the lack of focus and the absence of a sense of strategy and tactics.

Even the most successful companies are rarely overnight successes. Instead, they tend to start small and solve the problems of a specific niche. Over time, they then expand to take over larger and larger portions of the market.

What I like to hear discussed in a pitch is both the size of the overall market and the size of the addressable or initial target market. I also do not want to hear that you expect to conquer a huge market in one fell swoop. Instead, I want to get the sense that you understand that you have to break a market up into a series of smaller, more bite-sized pieces.

Looking Naive – Along those lines, one of the biggest mistakes people make is looking naïve. I can't tell you how many times people have said to me, completely sincerely...

- This idea can't miss!
- This is a business that cannot fail!
- If we can get just 1 percent of the market...
- This thing will sell itself!
- We have no competition!

Instead of getting me excited about their Solution, what statements like those do is convince me that the team either does not understand how hard it is to get people to change, does not understand the concept of substitutes, or hasn't done any basic market research.

Excessive Hype – When you are delivering your pitch, it is important that you are enthusiastic. However, it is just as important that you look realistic. The reason is that many people operate according to the rule that if something sounds too good to be true, it probably is. As a result, if you lay on the hype too thick, you run the risk of looking like you are naïve, exaggerating, or both. Instead, you want to strike a balance; to look excited, enthusiastic, and confident but also aware of the risks you face.

The Tease – Some people try to use a tease strategy with their elevator pitch. They figure they will try to intrigue the audience by not really saying anything and make the audience want to let them in on the secret. While this approach works with movies and books, it doesn't work with elevator pitches. When going to a movie or reading a book, people expect – and want – to be teased. That's what they are paying for. However, when listening to an elevator pitch, people expect you to give them a basic set of information without their having to work very hard for it. The harder you make it for people to understand what you are talking about, the more likely they are to just ignore you.

The Hard Sell – One of the first rules of sales is to ask for the sale; to try to close the sale then and there. While this works when you are selling some products, it doesn't work when you are delivering an elevator pitch. As I explain in the Conversational chapter, an elevator pitch is just a part of a larger process and there's no way to rush the process since part of the goal is to build a relationship with the other party.

The Crazy Eddie – Some people take enthusiasm to the extreme and deliver a hyperkinetic, high-energy pitch in which they jump and storm around the stage. While this approach may appeal to some people, it is unlikely to work with venture capitalists and senior business executives. They tend to be thoughtful, conservative, and pragmatic people who value emotion and enthusiasm, but not in excess.

Looking too Slick – While it's important that you look polished and professional, you don't want to look too slick. A good team is made up of both business people who know how to present a solid image and technical people who are a little rough around the edges but who know how to get things done. It always makes me nervous if a team looks like it's full of salespeople and no technical people, because it makes me wonder about their ability to deliver on their promises.

Asking for too Little Money – Asking for too little money can be worse than asking for too much money because it can make you look naïve. I once worked with a life science start-up that seemed to think that they could get to market for a total investment of less than $500,000. The truth is that it is hard to bring a life science product to market for less than $5 million and by asking for so little money the team left potential investors wondering whether they actually knew what they were doing.

Blanking Out – When delivering your elevator pitch, nothing will destroy your credibility faster than blanking out; completely forgetting what you were going to say. I have only seen this happen a few times, but they are some of the most memorably awkward moments of my life. As a result, I recommend that when delivering your pitch to a large audience for the first time, you have with you a copy of your elevator pitch that you can just read from if all else fails.

Reading from a Script – While reading from a script is better than blanking out, it is only slightly better. If you stand up on stage with your nose buried in a sheet of paper, you are going to look like a geek who needs serious marketing help (and who may not know it or want it).

Going Long – Many organizations hold elevator pitch forums in which people are given a minute or two to deliver their pitch. Few things bother me more than when people go over their allotted time during these events. Going long says two things to me, neither of which is good. First, going long says that you are unprepared and disorganized; that you haven't bothered to rehearse your pitch and get the timing right. Second, going long makes you look self-centered and says that you don't respect anyone else's time, including the audience's and the other presenters' time.

Going long can be a problem even if there is no preset limit to the length of your pitch. If I were to meet a venture capitalist in a social setting, I would still try to limit my elevator pitch to two minutes. The reason is that keeping things concise makes you look professional and respectful of their time. If the venture capitalist wants to keep talking, then great. However, you don't want to tie them up for half an hour and force them to listen to a pitch that they have no interest in because that will dramatically decrease the odds that they will speak positively of you to their friends, some of whom may actually be interested in your Solution.

Breathlessness – I don't care how desperate you may actually be; when delivering your pitch, you simply can't look desperate. That means that you have to cut your pitch down to the absolute minimum number of words so that you can deliver it in a relaxed manner. Delivering your pitch in a relaxed manner will also help you look organized and professional.

CREDIBILITY BUILDERS

Now that I've talked about the things that will damage your credibility, let me talk about the things that will build up your credibility. These are listed in roughly their descending order of persuasiveness.

Paying Customers – The best way to establish your credibility is to find a paying customer. That doesn't mean people who have expressed an interest in your Solution or who are willing to test it for free. Instead, that means people who are willing to actually write you a check or, better yet, people who have actually written you a check.

Prior Experience With the Customer and the Problem – If you don't have a paying customer, then the next best credibility builder is relevant experience in the category or market. What relevant experience does is suggest that you know what you are talking about and that what you say is actually true.

Experienced Management Team – If you don't have direct experience with the customer and the problem, then the next best thing is general experience. Very often, general experience will help a team make the adjustments that have to be made as an idea inevitably morphs over time.

Patents – Obtaining patents and other forms of intellectual property protection will help to establish your credibility because they provide an independent validation that your Solution is at least unique. However, they are of only limited value because investors know that being unique won't automatically translate into success in the marketplace.

Memorizing and Rehearsing Your Pitch – The best elevator pitches are the ones that are memorized and carefully rehearsed, but don't look it. In my experience, you have to deliver a pitch 20 to 30 times before you start to get comfortable enough with it that you can deliver it without thinking about it (which enables you to pay attention to how it's going over with the audience).

Dressing the Part – As I explained to my son when he was 11 and wanted to make the "A" baseball team at his school, it isn't enough to know what you're doing. Instead, you also have to look like you know what you are doing. Just as he needed to look like a baseball player at the evaluations, when delivering your elevator pitch you need to look like you can fit into the business world. That doesn't mean that you have to go overboard, but you do want to look professional. At a minimum, that means wearing a nice pair of pants or a skirt, a button-down shirt, and a blazer or sport coat.

4.5. CONCEPTUAL

> *"A fool uttereth all his mind."*
> – Proverbs 29:11

While I enjoy playing the game of golf, it also tends to drive me crazy. The problem is that I have a tendency to pick my head up a fraction of a second before the point of contact. As result, I occasionally "top" the ball, hitting it with tremendous topspin and sending it scurrying down the fairway just inches above the grass. My father has a wonderful and vivid term that he uses to describe a ball hit like this.

He calls it a "worm burner."

I love this concept so much that I use it to describe a type of elevator pitch. Just as a worm burner in the context of golf is a shot that hugs the ground, a worm burner in the context of an elevator pitch is a pitch that starts out – and stays at – an extremely low level. Rather than giving a 30,000-foot overview of a Solution, a worm burner quickly gets into operational, technical, and other unnecessary details.

The problem with a worm burner is that, because no effort is made to first establish the context of the Solution that is being pitched and what is being said, in most cases all of that detail goes right over the head of the audience and leaves them wondering what you are talking about.

DON'T GET LOST IN THE HOW

Worm burners are a particular problem when it comes to engineers, programmers, scientists, and other very smart, very technical people. The problem is that they spend so much of their lives dealing with the HOW of their Solution – HOW it should work, HOW to get it to work, and HOW to make it – that they end up getting lost in the HOW.

An example of HOW-focused thinking is represented by this quote from inventor Dean Kamen...

> People used to tell me that if you can't explain your idea in the span of an elevator ride, then it's not a good idea.
> My answer?
> If I have an idea that I could explain completely in an elevator, it ain't much of an idea.

There is certainly some truth to what Dean Kamen is saying. A good innovation has to have some magic, secret sauce, miracle, or other unfair advantage behind it. Otherwise, it will be too easy to copy and compete with.

However, Dean Kamen completely misses the point when it comes to an elevator pitch. That is made clear by his use of the word "completely" in the last sentence of his quote.

Your elevator pitch is not the time to get into the details of your magic, secret sauce, miracle, or other unfair advantage.

For one thing, there isn't enough time. You also don't want to make it too easy for people to rip you off by spilling all of your secrets in your elevator pitch.

Instead, the point of an elevator pitch is to just give the audience a basic, high-level understanding of your Solution. If the audience is interested, then you can get into all of the low-level details at a later date and in a more appropriate setting.[6]

THE EXAMPLE OF SALESLOGIX

In terms of SalesLogix, our Solution was made possible by multiple pieces of technical magic. These included the ability to modify the application at run time and our database synchronization technology. However, when it came to the SalesLogix elevator pitch, we only touched on those things but didn't get into the details of them...

> In contrast, SalesLogix delivers the best of both worlds...
> • The affordability and ease of use of a contact manager.
> • The scalability, database synchronization, customization, and reporting capabilities of a high-end CRM system.

In general, the SalesLogix elevator pitch focused on WHAT our system did and WHY people needed it rather than HOW it did what it did. That is one reason why it was so effective.

THE PROPER SEQUENCE

Most people will either never care about the HOW of your Solution or they will only care about the HOW of your Solution after you first explain...

What...Is It?
Who...Needs It?
Why...Do They Need It?
WhoRU...To See The Problem And Build The Solution?

Only after answering those much more basic questions, and establishing the context of your Solution, should you even think about getting into the HOW of your Solution.

WHAT

When presented with any idea, the first questions the audience will ask – explicitly or not – are the Whatzit questions...

• What is it?
• What is it like?

People do not process new information in a vacuum; instead, they tend to relate new things to what they already know. That enables them to more quickly make sense of and put to use what they learn.

The easiest way to explain the WHAT of your Solution is to give a plain-English definition of it and then explain what your Solution is like. Of course, you then have to explain how and why your Solution is different than the state of the art.

WHO

Once you have explained WHAT your Solution is, you must then explain WHO needs it...

• Who will use it?
• Who will buy it?
• To Whom does it apply?

Touching on the WHO of your Solution in your elevator pitch is important because it makes it clear that you have some sense of the customer and are not talking about a Solution In Search Of A Problem (SISOAP).

WHY

Of course, it isn't enough to explain WHO needs your Solution; you must also explain WHY they need it. You must explain the problem; the thing that is wrong with the state of the art and that will drive people to abandon their existing solution and change and adopt your Solution.

WHORU

Explaining the WHORU of your innovation involves establishing your credibility. Most people – including investors, executive sponsors, and customers – will only pay attention to what you say if you can convince them that you know what you are talking about; that you understand the problem and are qualified to build the solution.

HOW

Only after you have established the WHAT, WHO, WHY, and WHORU of your Solution should you even consider getting into HOW your Solution works. The logic is that if the audience understands the WHAT, WHO, WHY, and WHORU of your Solution, then they will usually tell you so and you can then just skip ahead to the HOW. However, if your audience doesn't understand them and you just skip over them and go straight to the HOW, they won't tell you that they're lost. Instead, they'll just smile and nod as if they are listening, but you'll never hear back from them.

HOW TO TELL WHAT FROM HOW

When creating an elevator pitch, it is important that you not go into too much unnecessary detail. The problem is that sometimes people have a hard time knowing where to draw the line. Let me give you a list of some things that are too HOW and that should be left out of an elevator pitch...

• Proprietary algorithms or formulae.
• Technical or operational details.
• Anything you would consider to be proprietary.
• Anything that should be discussed only after signing a Non-Disclosure Agreement (NDA).

4.6. CONCRETE

> *"Perhaps the efforts of the true poets, founders, religious, literatures, all ages, have been ... to bring people back from their persistent strayings and sickly abstractions, to the costless, average, divine, original concrete."* – Walt Whitman

A few years ago, I worked for a start-up called Rogue Research.[7] We were doing something very cutting edge and revolutionary; building an entirely new model of application development and deployment. The problem was that we were having a hard time raising large chunks of money from venture capitalists. Instead, we had to spend much more time talking to angel investors and raising more, smaller chunks of money from them. While this financing strategy ultimately worked, it made things a little more exciting than they needed to be. This led to some disruptive turnover as a few people were forced to take jobs that were less risky.

Over the years, I have spent a non-trivial amount of time trying to figure out why we had such a hard time attracting the attention of venture capitalists. Recently, I came to understand that the problem wasn't just with who we were but with how we were presenting ourselves to venture capitalists and other professional investors.

HOW PROFESSIONAL INVESTORS THINK

Professional investors – and venture capitalists in particular – do not like two things...
- Waiting
- Risk

When it comes to waiting, the reality is that professional investors generally cannot afford to invest in ventures that do not offer at least the hope of paying out in 3 to 5 years. As a result, they usually will not back a product or service that is more than 12 months away from being launched.

Professional investors also, and contrary to many peoples' perceptions, generally don't like risk. Sure, they are in the business of placing bets, but by and large those are calculated bets. Instead, professional investors only invest in ventures where the risks can be managed.

AN INCOMPATIBLE MESSAGE

A year or so ago I came to realize that the problem that we ran into at Rogue Research was that the way we were presenting ourselves to venture capitalists was almost the exact opposite of what we needed to do to get their attention. That is because the message we were putting forth made us look anything but concrete.

First, the name of the company included the word "research." While the CEO had very valid reasons for liking this name, the reality was that the word "research," rather than making us look concrete and business-like, instead made us look a little too academic (and thus more risky). The problem is that pure research companies often don't make anything. Instead, they tend to make their money by licensing their technology. While this can be a very profitable business model (think Dolby Labs), it can also take a very long time for the cash to start flowing.

Second, most of the people on the team had a very technical bent and were more focused on what was going on deep inside the product, rather than the surface of the product. The result was that it took us a long time to come up with a truly compelling demonstration – or "demo" – of the product. Instead, our demo wasn't visual enough, relied too much on the assumed technical knowledge of the audience, and left too much up to the imagination. Consequently, while our demo did its job in some ways, it did not do as much as it could to help us raise money.

THINGS THAT HELP YOU LOOK CONCRETE

As a result of my experience at Rogue Research and a series of other start-ups, I have come to believe that if you want to improve your ability to secure financial and/or other backing for your Solution, your elevator pitch must make it clear that your Solution is concrete; that it can be turned into a real product or service in a relatively short period of time.

In other words, you must make it clear that you are more than just a couple of people with a good idea.

Listed below are some things you can do that will help communicate to the audience that what you are doing is concrete, rather than abstract and academic.

Talk About Products, Not Technologies – One way to send the message that you are concrete is to use terms like "product" and "service" and avoid terms like "idea" and "technology." By speaking – and thinking – in these more concrete terms, you will make it clear to potential backers that you understand the need to deliver value in a relatively short period of time.

If all you have is an idea or a raw technology, you must focus your efforts on turning it into a tangible product or service; something that somebody would want to buy right now (or fairly soon) and not something that somebody might want to buy at some point in the future.

That also means that if you are still years away from having something that can be commercialized, you shouldn't waste your time talking to venture capitalists. Instead, you should target friends, family, angel investors, and others who are more patient and more willing to take a risk.

Develop a Good Demo – One of the things that really helped sell SalesLogix to investors, business partners, and customers was that we focused on making sure that our product was demo-able at a very early stage in the process. Instead of building the product from the inside out, and putting the initial focus on the inner workings of the product, we instead built the product from the outside-in. That meant that from the beginning of the process we spent a tremendous amount of time nailing down things like the product's user interface. As a result, very early on in the process of building SalesLogix we were able to give people a reasonable sense of how the product was going to look and work, which made it much easier to sell.

Discuss Demonstrable Accomplishments – There is nothing more concrete than actually getting things done. As a result, your pitch should mention anything that you have accomplished. This includes things like raising angel money or shipping early versions of your product.

Recruit an Experienced Management Team – Venture capitalists generally prefer to back good teams more than good ideas. This is because they know that in many cases the initial version of the idea will not pan out and the team must shift its focus and find a different problem to solve.

Sign Up Alpha or Beta Customers – The sooner you can get Ordinary People using and testing out your Solution, the better. As a result, when developing their products, software companies usually do both Alpha and Beta release. An Alpha release is a version of the product that is known to be very buggy but that still demonstrates the basic functionality of the system. Once most of the major features have been implemented, software companies then start releasing Beta versions of their product, which help people start to get familiar with the product (and to do some free testing).

Be Specific – One way to make your Solution look concrete is to be specific. Instead of just talking about general trends like how the population is aging or people are getting fatter, you should instead talk about the specific problems of specific products and how they fail to meet the needs of specific customers.

Quantifiable Benefits – The more specific and quantifiable you can be about the benefits of your Solution, the better. That means being specific and quantifiable about how you are faster, better, and/or cheaper. That also means talking about benefits in terms of things like time, money, or lives saved.

Focus Your Efforts – One of the biggest mistakes people make when selling an idea for a new product or service is not being focused. Instead of trying to solve one problem that is affecting a specific group of people, they try to sell multiple products to multiple, and very different, audiences. The problem is that it is extremely difficult, if not impossible, for a new team to solve multiple problems of different customers at once. As a result, lack of focus is one thing that will tend to scare off professional investors.

4.7. CONSISTENT

> *"Look to make your course regular, that men may know beforehand what they may expect."*
> – Francis Bacon

One thing I never understood early on in my career – when I spent all of my time on the entrepreneur's side of the table – was what venture capitalists, angel investors, executives, and others did after hearing a pitch. Not knowing any better, I assumed they made their decisions pretty much on their own.

However, as I started to make friends in the venture capital community, and started judging pitches at Washington University in St. Louis, I developed a very different view of the process. That view drove home to me the value of ensuring that an elevator pitch is consistent.

The way the process actually works is that almost every potential investor, executive, or backer is a specialist in some specific area, be it finance, technology, or marketing. Very few potential investors, executives, or backers actually have a deep understanding of all the different areas that are involved in putting together a successful new product, service, or other Solution. As a result, the smart ones compensate for the holes in their knowledge by building up networks of people that they can go to and whose opinions they trust.

I saw this happen first-hand in 1999 during the heart of the dot-com boom. One of my friends is a venture capitalist. He is an expert when it comes to the world of finance and deal structuring, but doesn't have a deep knowledge of technology or new product development. As a result, when looking at a potential deal, he would ask me to have breakfast with him and would explain the deal to me and ask me for my technical and general opinion of it. I would then give him my opinion of the technical feasibility of the idea and the general feasibility of the idea (i.e. whether it addressed a problem that was causing significant amounts of pain).

THE BENEFITS OF CONSISTENCY

Given that powerful people are constantly talking to each other, you must be sure that everyone hears the same basic message.

When I am working to balance out the requirements of making an elevator pitch both consistent and customized, I try to make sure that 80 percent of the content is pretty much the same between the different versions of the pitch. That means that I usually start out with the same summary sentence and body text, but customize the close of the pitch. The benefit of sticking with the 80 percent commonality rule of thumb is that if someone hears a version of your elevator pitch that isn't targeted directly at them – if for example a potential investor hears the employee-oriented version of your elevator pitch – they will still understand what you are talking about.

All of this emphasis on creating an elevator pitch that is both consistent and customized is important because at the end of the day word of mouth is an extremely important and powerful tool. The more attention you pay to crafting a message that can be easily spread from one person to the next – and the more you focus on turning your audience into your salesforce – the faster and better your message will spread. This is because people tend to place much more trust in messages that they hear from people they know than they do from sources like advertising.

BEYOND THE SUMMARY SENTENCE

With that in mind, let me give you a sense of how to flow out an elevator pitch in a way that allows you to satisfy the need for your elevator pitch to be consistent but also customizable...

Summary Sentence
_____

The Customer
The Problem
The Pain
The Competition
The Solution
The Features
The Benefits
The Team
The Objective
_____

The Deal
The Technology

We largely followed this flow in the SalesLogix elevator pitch that I have discussed earlier, so let me explain this flow in the context of that pitch.

The Customer – Early on in your elevator pitch, it is important that you give the audience a sense of who your target customer is.

One thing this will do is help explain the WHAT of your innovation. It will also help you look more focused and thus more concrete.

I can't tell you how many pitches I have heard that focus on the Solution and completely ignore the customer. Pitches like these make me extremely nervous because they make me wonder whether the team actually understands basic, but critical, things like sales and marketing or whether they think their Solution will sell itself.

When it came to the SalesLogix elevator pitch, our target customer was generally mid-sized (or middle market) organizations. As a result, in our customer statement we made that explicit by using the phrase "mid-sized companies." We also helped to establish who our target customer was by using the phrase CRM and by naming our two chief competitors…

> *SalesLogix is targeting mid-sized companies that have outgrown contact managers like Act but can't afford the cost and complexity of high-end CRM products like Siebel.*

The Problem – Experienced venture capitalists, executives, and other backers understand that for your Solution to have a good chance of succeeding, it is important that it solves a problem. As a result, when listening to an elevator pitch, they will be on the lookout for evidence that your Solution is built around a good problem.

The best way to deal with this requirement is to explicitly discuss the problem your Solution solves in the body of your elevator pitch. You should do this around the same time you discuss the customer, because in most cases the problem and the customer are intertwined.

One way to explain the problem your Solution solves is by explaining what is wrong with the state of the art, and a good way to do that is with the word "too." By "too," I mean that you should establish that the state of the art is too slow, too expensive, too heavy, too big, too time-consuming, or something like that.

When it came to SalesLogix, the problem wasn't that there weren't any solutions to the problem. There were. Rather, the problem was that existing solutions forced customers to make an impossible choice between usability and power…

The problem with existing CRM solutions is that they fall into one of two categories. On the one hand, you have contact managers like Act that salespeople love but that do not allow people to share information across a large organization. On the other hand you have high-end CRM systems like Siebel that scale to support the needs of hundreds or thousands of users but that sales-people refuse to use.

We created SalesLogix to solve that problem; to give organizations a system that was both easy to use and powerful.

The Pain – While solving a problem is extremely important, it isn't enough to guarantee that your Solution will be successful. That is because in many cases it is easier, and less risky, for people to just deal with the pain that is caused by the state of the art than it is for them to endure the pain, and take on the risk, of switching to a new product or solution.

As a result, what you need to provide in your elevator pitch is evidence of the pain; evidence that the state of the art is so badly broken that it makes more sense for the customer to switch to a new solution.

Sometimes it is helpful to think of the pain as the consequence of the problem; as the cost of the pain put in terms of time or money. It then makes sense to discuss the pain in those concrete terms. However, if the customer already understands the pain they are in, and is simply looking for a solution to it, then you can discuss the pain at a more conceptual level. That is what we did in the SalesLogix elevator pitch...

The result is that too many organizations are unable to...

• Coordinate their sales and customer service teams.
• Obtain a holistic picture of the customer.
• Maximize the revenue gained from each customer.

One thing to notice about this part of the SalesLogix elevator pitch is that, because the buyers of our product (sales managers) weren't necessarily the same as the users of our product (salespeople), we slanted our characterization of the pain so that it would resonate more with the buyer of our product than the user. In other words, we explained the pain in the context of the sales manager's job and not the salesperson's job.

The Competition – Too few elevator pitches mention the competition. While this is understandable, the problem is that ignoring the competition can do several things.

First, ignoring the competition can damage your credibility; it can make people worry that you are so naïve as to think that you don't have any competition. Second, not mentioning the competition can make the audience wonder whether you have done your homework. Third, not mentioning the competition can make the audience wonder whether an opportunity actually exists. While in some cases the absence of competition points to a huge opportunity, in other cases it can indicate that the problem simply isn't worth solving.

In the SalesLogix elevator pitch, we mentioned the competition on multiple occasions...

> *SalesLogix is targeting mid-sized companies that have outgrown contact managers like Act but can't afford the cost and complexity of high-end CRM products like Siebel.*

However, in mentioning the competition we also made it clear what was wrong with the state of the art. The competition was not perfect, which created the opportunity that we saw.

The Solution, the Features, and the Benefits – Once you have established both the problem and the pain, then it's time to revisit your Solution and explain WHAT it is in slightly greater detail, usually in the context of features and benefits. A good rule of thumb to follow when doing this is to never mention a feature without tying it to a benefit.

Discussing your Solution and its features in the context of the benefits it delivers is important because it improves the likelihood that the audience will remember what you are saying. Instead of simply loading them down with facts, by also discussing the benefits you are giving the audience the context they need to appreciate and remember what you are saying.

The best place to look for benefits is in your statement of what's wrong with the state of the art. The benefits you must deliver in order to be successful are the opposite of what's wrong with the state of the art.

If the state of the art is expensive, you must be affordable. If the state of the art is slow, you must be fast. If the state of the art is cumbersome, you must be easy to use.

Where possible, when it comes to talking about benefits it is best to describe them in times of either money or time. That means explaining how a feature will help the customer make money, save money, or save time.

When it came to the SalesLogix elevator pitch, we stuck with a higher-level explanation of the benefits of our product. This was because we knew that customers were going to be using SalesLogix to replace an existing, unsatisfactory system. As a result, we knew the audience could compute the value of the benefits themselves...

> In contrast, SalesLogix delivers the best of both worlds...
> • The affordability and ease of use of a contact manager.
> • The scalability, database synchronization, customization, and reporting capabilities of a high-end CRM system.

The Team – Too many elevator pitches either spend too little – and in many cases absolutely no – time talking about the team or they don't talk about the aspects of a team that really matter. This is a problem because the team is often the first thing potential investors and backers consider when it comes to judging whether to invest or not.

As a result, toward the end of your elevator pitch you must mention the qualifications of your team to see the problem and to build the solution. This doesn't mean you need to name each individual person. Only do that if a person's experience is especially impressive or relevant. Instead, in most cases it is enough to add up how much total experience you have in the market you are targeting.

This is what we did in the SalesLogix elevator pitch. We explicitly named our CEO and his experience because it was so important for establishing our credibility. However, we also gave a hint of the overall depth of experience of the team as a whole, without spending too much time doing so...

> The SalesLogix team has over 75 years of combined experience in the industry and is led by Pat Sullivan, the co-founder and former CEO of Contact Software International, the original developer of Act.

The Objective – As I explain in the Customized chapter, while an effective elevator pitch is generally consistent across its different versions, it must also be customized so that it addresses the interests of the audience. The place to do most of that customization is in the objective. For example, a customer-oriented version of an elevator pitch will have a very different objective (sometimes asking for a next step or even the sale) than will an investor-oriented elevator pitch.

In the case of the version of the SalesLogix elevator pitch I discuss in this book, it was focused on raising money from venture capitalists. As a result, it mentioned how much money we needed and what we intended to use that money for, which we knew were the main things venture capitalists would be interested in...

> *SalesLogix is seeking $5 million to finance the continued development and marketing of SalesLogix 1.0, which is scheduled to be released in April 1997.*

In contrast, the customer-focused version of the SalesLogix elevator pitch closed differently, with a call to action and a reiteration of the positioning of SalesLogix...

> *We invite you to meet with us afterwards and learn more about SalesLogix, the first true CRM solution that's as easy to use as Act.*

Notice how this customer-focused closing statement is consistent with the positioning statement that we used in all of our marketing materials.

The Deal and the Technology – While some people think an elevator pitch should address such things as valuation, I believe that an effective elevator pitch leaves the deal and the technology (e.g. the HOW of your Solution) to later conversations. When it comes to the deal, things like valuation and capital structure are details that can and should be determined or negotiated at a later point, which makes it pointless – and a waste of precious time – to discuss them in your elevator pitch. When it comes to the technology, operational details, and other HOW-oriented elements, you simply do not have time to do them justice, so it's best to not address them at all in your elevator pitch.

In the case of the SalesLogix elevator pitch, we didn't lay out our product marketing strategies and tactics. Instead, all we mentioned was how much money we needed and what we planned to do with it at a high level...

> *SalesLogix is seeking $5 million to finance the continued development and marketing of SalesLogix 1.0, which is scheduled to be released in April 1997.*

Similarly, in the SalesLogix elevator pitch we didn't get into the HOW of our Solution. Instead, we just mentioned some high-level features...

> *In contrast, SalesLogix delivers the best of both worlds...*
>
> *• The affordability and ease of use of a contact manager.*
> *• The scalability, database synchronization, customization, and reporting capabilities of a high-end CRM system.*

We didn't get into the corresponding benefits because we knew they would be self-evident to the audience to whom we were speaking. We also knew that we alluded to the benefits of our system when we talked about the pain.

4.8. CUSTOMIZED

> *"The biggest single barrier to the development of an effective strategy is the strongly held belief that a company has to appeal to the entire market."*
>
> – Al Ries

A few years ago, I worked for a start-up that was headed up by an uber-geek. He lived, ate, and breathed technology. While this was great for the product, it caused some problems for us when it came to getting our message out.

The problem was that our CEO liked to think of himself as an Everyman – as just like everyone else – when in truth he was very different than most people.

This misconception came to a head one day when we were discussing the presentation he was to give to an audience of potential investors. I was happy with the presentation because it had worked several times before with angel investors, but the CEO wasn't. He wanted to change what we were saying and how we said it and go back to a lower level, more technical message that I knew didn't work with Ordinary People. I asked him why he wanted to make those changes, and he replied with something that has stuck with me ever since.

"It just doesn't work for me."

I have to admit to having a George Costanza, "Jerk Store" moment. Rather than coming back with a great line, I just sat there stunned when what I should have said is this.

"It doesn't matter."

At the end of the day, it didn't matter that the pitch didn't work for him because he wasn't the target audience. He was going to be giving the presentation to a non-technical audience.

What we needed was a message that would resonate with the audience, not the presenter.

DON'T JUDGE YOUR ELEVATOR PITCH BY YOUR OWN STANDARDS

When helping people and companies with their elevator pitches, I frequently encounter this problem. Instead of judging their elevator pitch by the standards of the audience, people instead judge their elevator pitch by their own standards. As a result, they end up with a pitch that is at best ineffective and at worst makes them look cut off from the real world.

This happens because people fail to realize that they are different than the audience; they are more interested in, and more knowledgeable about, their Solution than are most people. As a result, they fail to understand that what is compelling to them probably isn't compelling to others.

THE POWER OF FOCUS

The way to solve this problem is to first understand that messages are most powerful when they are focused; that the more focused a message is, the more powerfully it will resonate with the audience.

One reason why Procter & Gamble is such a large and powerful company is because they clearly understand this principle. Rather than trying to create one-size-fits-all products, they instead create different brands to solve different – and specific – problems. In fact, in some cases Procter & Gamble will have multiple brands in the same category (e.g. Cheer and Tide), seemingly competing with each other. However, the truth is that, since those products are positioned differently, those products aren't really competing against each other. Instead, they are appealing to different people with different problems.

General Motors used to understand this principle. When GM was in its heyday, it created a hierarchy of brands, each of which was designed to appeal to a different market. Chevrolet was the entry-level brand, Pontiac was the sporty brand, Cadillac was the high-end brand, and Buick and Oldsmobile were upper middle class brands. However, during the 80s GM largely abandoned this approach and tried to make every brand appeal to everyone. The result was that GM soon started to lose market share to Japanese companies who started to beat them with better quality but also, and just as importantly, used a hierarchical brand model (e.g. Honda/Acura and Toyota/Lexus/Scion).

WHAT EACH AUDIENCE WANTS TO HEAR

The same basic principle applies to creating an effective elevator pitch. One reason why elevator pitches often get long, and as a result less effective, is because people try to make them be everything to all people.

They try to appeal to everyone with a one-size-fits-all elevator pitch.

A far more effective strategy is to create (slightly) different versions of your elevator pitch, each of which is designed to appeal to a different audience. Each of those different versions should be generally similar but should stress slightly different things, especially when it comes to the close of the pitch.

Team Members – The first version of your elevator pitch that you need to develop is the one that you will use to sell your Solution to potential members of your team.

Team-focused elevator pitches are often inspirational and commonly stress the team's vision and their desire to change the world. Team-focused elevator pitches are also often lower-level – in other words more HOW – than are later versions of one's elevator pitch. This is because the target audience of a team-focused elevator pitch is generally people who already have some understanding of the technology and market.

That's why you want them to join your team. This team-focused elevator pitch is usually the easiest one for entrepreneurs to write because it usually requires the least amount of thought on their part. In most cases, you are looking for people pretty much like you. As a result, you can judge the quality of your pitch by whether it appeals to you or not.

Of course, the thing that often trips people up is that the initial, team-focused version of their elevator pitch often works quite well when it comes to recruiting. However, at some point – usually as people start trying to raise money – it stops working. This is because investors will be interested in your Solution for different reasons than will potential members of your team.

Investors, Backers, and/or Sponsors – The second version of your elevator pitch that you need to develop is one that is targeted at potential investors. This can include venture capitalists, angel investors, executive sponsors, and other backers.

A good investor-focused elevator pitch is different from a team-focused elevator pitch in a number of ways. First, a good investor-focused elevator pitch deals less with the HOW of your Solution and more with the WHAT and WHY. This is because potential investors will want to understand the value that your Solution will deliver and why people will change and adopt it. Investors are also unlikely to have much experience with, or interest in, the HOW of your thing. Second, a good Investor-focused elevator pitch more directly addresses the risks that are involved in bringing your Solution to life. As a result, a good investor-focused elevator pitch pays more attention to the WHORU factors that establish your credibility. That includes your qualifications to see the problem and to build the solution.

When writing an investor-focused elevator pitch, you need to keep in mind that there are a number of different types of venture capitalists and angel investors, all of whom are looking for, and invest in, different things. As a result, you can keep from wasting people's time – and look more knowledgeable and thus credible in the process – if you make several things clear in your pitch.

First, your pitch should make it clear what type of company you are; whether you are a service provider or a product company, a life sciences company or a technology start-up, and a hardware or software company. Second, your pitch should explain what stage you are in; whether you are an early-stage company that is looking for seed money or whether you are a going concern that needs help scaling your operations. Third, your pitch should explain how much money you need and what you need it for; whether you need it to finance the development of your product or for working capital.

Business Partners – In many cases, you cannot go to market by yourself. Instead, you have to recruit a team of people and companies who will help you. This can include Business Partners (BPs) like Value-Added Resellers (VARs), dealers, sales agents, and retailers.

When it comes to developing the BP-focused version of your elevator pitch, the thing to explain is why your product will be in demand; why it will sell. This is because, while business partners want you to be successful, first and foremost they are concerned with themselves.

This means that your BP-focused pitch should address the same credibility-based issues that you address in the investor-focused version of your elevator pitch. However, you also need to stress that you are a good group of people to work with. People do not want to partner with someone who will let them down. As a result, you need to stress your experience and your ability to do what you say you can do.

Press and Analysts – One of the cheapest, but most powerful, ways to build awareness about your Solution is to take advantage of the power of the press. Because of the press's inherent credibility – and the fact that what others say about you is always more powerful than what you say about yourself – a single well-placed article can do more for you than hundreds of thousands, or even millions, of dollars spent on advertising.

There are several things to keep in mind when you are working with the press and analysts, and in particular the business press.

First, the press needs you; they are constantly having to find new content to fill up their newspapers, magazines, and blogs. However, at the same time the press is trying to serve their readers by providing them with high-quality news and information. As a result, the press and analysts are highly concerned with the credibility of the sources they rely on.

They need to feel confident that what they say or write about is the truth.

A second thing to keep in mind when it comes to the press and analysts is that they are always trying to get ahead of their competition. As a result, they are always interested in a new and different vision of the future.

However, that vision has to be backed up with significant credibility – significant evidence as to why it's true – before they will buy into it.

Customers – The last version of your elevator pitch that you need to develop is your Customer-focused pitch. Fortunately, this isn't too hard to do because potential customers are concerned about the same basic things as potential investors. They want to understand the value and benefits your Solution will deliver and why you will be able to get the job done.

HOW THIS WORKED AT SALESLOGIX

While the SalesLogix pitch was generally consistent across the different audiences to which we delivered it, we would change the ending of the pitch and some of the things that we emphasized depending on to whom we were speaking.

SalesLogix Investor Pitch – The version of the SalesLogix elevator pitch that we delivered to potential investors focused almost exclusively on the credibility of the team. Rather than getting into too much detail about the problem, we instead explained that it was a problem with which we had been familiar for a number of years.

SalesLogix Business Partner Pitch – The version of the SalesLogix elevator pitch that we delivered to potential business partners focused on the specific problem of database synchronization, because we knew that was the Achilles Heel of every existing solution and the thing that was driving Value-Added Resellers (VARs) crazy. Everyone said that they had solved the problem of database synchronization, but the VARs knew from personal experience that they hadn't. We knew there was no point in getting into too much detail about all the different features that our product provided if we didn't first establish that we knew how to solve that biggest problem of them all. We also knew that if we could convince potential business partners that we had solved the problem of database synchronization, then they would regard all the other features of the product as gravy.

SalesLogix Press and Analyst Pitch – The version of the SalesLogix elevator pitch that we delivered to members of the press and analysts focused on several things. First and foremost, we focused on the credibility of the team, because that gave immediate weight to our observations about the market. What was a little different about this version of our elevator pitch was that we got a little more into what George Bush The Elder would call, "The Vision Thing." We did this because we knew that analysts tend to be interested in the different vendors' visions of where the market is going.

HOW THIS WORKED AT ROGUE RESEARCH

The Rogue Research elevator pitch also followed pretty much the same pattern as the SalesLogix elevator pitch. It was generally consistent but could be customized depending on which audience we were speaking to.

As we first started to go public with what we were doing, our primary needs were for additional team-members and technical business partners who could build solutions using the tool we had created. As a result, we created a summary sentence that was fairly HOW-focused...

> *Rogue Research is a software company and makes a software product, called Cloud Creator, that enables large numbers of commodity computers to form a mission critical computing environment called a Cloud.*

While this version worked well when given to a technical audience that was already familiar with concepts like clustering and application servers, it didn't work as well with less technical audiences like potential investors. That is because it didn't explicitly point out the benefits of what we were doing. As a result, as the target audience of our elevator pitch changed, we also changed our summary sentence...

> *Rogue Research is a software company and makes a software product, called Cloud Creator, that enables businesses and other organizations to drive down the cost of mission critical computing.*

This version of our summary sentence gave the audience enough sense of what we were building – a software product – but also was much clearer when it came to the benefits our product would deliver.

WHEN AND WHAT TO CUSTOMIZE

When it comes to customizing your elevator pitch, there are a couple of things to keep in mind.

First, it is important that you keep your summary sentence fairly consistent. You want your summary sentence to be understandable by the widest possible range of people since, in many situations, it may be all that you have time to say.

Second, most customization should be done in the close of your elevator pitch. You want to make sure that everyone has the same basic understanding of what you are doing and why. However, since the last thing you say will tend to linger with the audience, you want the last thing you say to be especially relevant to them.

THE MIXED OR MYSTERY AUDIENCE

While you should always strive to use the version of your elevator pitch that is the best fit with the interests of the audience, this isn't always easy to do. In some cases, you may not know who is in the audience. In other cases, the audience may be made up of a mixture of potential investors, partners, customers, or all three.

What should you do?

If you don't know who is in the audience, or the audience is made up of a mix of people, then the thing to do is to use the version of your elevator pitch that targets the people with whom you most need to speak at the moment.

If you are very early on in the process and are still trying to put your Solution together, then the version to use is the employee-focused version of your elevator pitch. If you have put your team together and your main need is money, then use the investor-focused version of your elevator pitch. If you have a team and money, then use the customer-focused version of your elevator pitch.

That way you will speak most directly and powerfully to members of the audience with which you most need to speak. However, since your elevator pitch isn't overly focused on one audience, the other members of the audience will still get a basic understanding of what you are doing and why.

4.9. CONVERSATIONAL

> *"One of the best ways to persuade others is with your ears; by listening to them."*
> – Dean Rusk

One of my favorite books is Stephen Covey's *The Seven Habits of Highly Effective People*. One of the key lessons of this book is that successful people begin with the end in mind. They know what they want to achieve before they start working. This helps them plan out what they are going to do before they get started. This also helps them monitor their progress along the way and make any adjustments that are necessary.

The problem is that it's hard to know what to do, and what the end looks like, if you don't understand what the process looks like. I believe that helps explain why so many elevator pitches are so long and/or ineffective (or just plain bad). Most people do not know what the process actually looks like, so they are just flying blind.

Let me try to shed a little light on things.

AN OVERVIEW OF THE PROCESS

If your elevator pitch was the only chance you had to convey your message to someone before they decided to back you – or not – then it would make sense to cram as much stuff into it as possible.

But that's not the case.

Instead of being the Alpha and the Omega of an investment decision, an elevator pitch is just one step in the process. Yes, it's an extremely important step, but at the end of the day you will have several other opportunities to tell – and to flesh out – your story.

At this point, all you want to do is get the audience's attention.

If you do manage to get a venture capitalist's attention with your elevator pitch, then they will probably ask to see your business plan. If the executive summary of your business plan appeals to them – and to their firm – then they will likely read the rest of your business plan. Assuming your business plan holds together, they will then ask you to come in and give a one-hour presentation. After that comes the whole due diligence process, during which they will finally be interested in getting into the HOW of your Solution.

What all of this means is that you shouldn't get ahead of yourself when creating or delivering your elevator pitch.

Instead of trying to close the deal then and there, your goal should be to just get to the next step; sending them your business plan or setting up a longer meeting.

RELATED PITCHES

The process is similar if you are selling a project within a large organization or trying to close the sale for a product or service. In neither case are you going to close the deal with your elevator pitch. Instead, you're going to have to attend at least one – and probably multiple – meetings. As a result, your goal should just be to interest the audience in what you have to say by explaining WHAT you are doing, WHY you are doing it, and WHORU.

THINK DIALOGUE, NOT MONOLOGUE

One problem that many people run into is that they get so focused on delivering their elevator pitch that they lose sight of the audience and its reaction to their pitch.

There isn't much you can do about this if you are delivering your pitch to a room full of people. However, if you are talking to just one or two people, you have the opportunity to judge how your elevator pitch is going over and customize it on the fly. To do that, you have to have your pitch memorized to the degree that you can be paying close attention to the reaction of the audience. Do they look like they are following your Elevator pitch or do they look lost?

ELEVATOR PITCH, NOT ELEVATOR SPEECH

Along the same lines, unlike some people I use the term "Elevator Pitch," rather than "Elevator Speech," because I think the word "Pitch" better communicates what you are trying to accomplish and how. A good pitch is an interactive, conversational thing while a speech is a one-way thing.

PAUSE DURING YOUR PITCH

Sometimes when I am delivering an elevator pitch to an individual, and especially if I don't know anything about the person to whom I am speaking, I will deliberately pause after I deliver my summary sentence and before I get into the body of my pitch. This is so that I can judge the reaction of the audience and so that they can interject something that may help me customize my pitch to their interests. The idea is to gain additional information that I can use to make the pitch more relevant and resonant with the audience.

SOFT SELL, NOT HARD SELL

One of the rules of selling is that you should always ask for the sale. While this makes sense in some circumstances, it doesn't work in the context of an elevator pitch.

As I said before, the point of an elevator pitch isn't to close the deal. Rather, the point of an elevator pitch is to just take the conversation to the next level.

If you try to close prematurely, you are more likely to turn the audience off than you are to turn them on. As a result, instead of asking for the sale at the end of your elevator pitch, ask for the opportunity to tell the audience more about who you are, what you are doing, and why.

5. FREQUENTLY MADE MISTAKES

"Only those who do nothing...make no mistakes."
– Joseph Conrad

As I have said multiple times before in this book, one way to make sure that people understand – and more importantly remember – your message is to be redundant. That means telling the audience what you are going to tell them, telling them, and then telling them what you told them. Toward that end, let me reiterate some of the key points of this book, in the form of the mistakes I most frequently see people make, in the hope that they will stick with you.

BURYING THE LEDE

As I said earlier on in this book, many newspapers structure their stories in the form of an inverted pyramid. In order to enable people to quickly get the gist of the story and determine whether it's relevant to them or not, they try to answer the Who, What, Where, When, and Why questions in the first paragraph, if not the first sentence, of the story.

Using the same basic approach will tend to make an elevator pitch easier to understand and remember. Unfortunately, in too many of the elevator pitches that I hear, the really important information – WHAT the Solution is, WHY people will adopt it, and WHORU – is buried amidst a mass of far less important information. This is a problem because, like the readers of a newspaper, the audience for an elevator pitch will often decide in the first few seconds whether the pitch is relevant to them and their interests and whether they should pay attention to it or not.

If you don't quickly let the audience know how your pitch relates to their interests and concerns, then they may just tune you out.

For this reason, I am not a fan of leading elevator pitches off with questions, stories, or jokes because they use up precious time that could be better spent establishing the WHAT, WHY, and WHORU of your Solution. However, the bigger problem with including questions, stories, or jokes in an elevator pitch is that they lengthen the time it takes you to establish your relevance to that audience. For that reason, if you insist on including a question, story, or joke in your elevator pitch, then I suggest that you place it after your summary sentence. That way your summary sentence will explain to the audience where you are going and make them more likely to pay attention to your entire pitch.

NOT ESTABLISHING YOUR CREDIBILITY

It is a well-established fact that between 75 and 90 percent of new businesses and new products fail. While that sometimes happens due to poor timing or bad luck, in most cases new business and products fail because they are fatally flawed; because they fail to take into account some basic and subtle, but critically important, truth about the marketplace.

One way that venture capitalists and executives try to manage this risk is by backing individuals and teams more than specific Solutions. They know that few plans survive the initial contact with the enemy, or the marketplace, and that an experienced team will know how to make the adjustments that are necessary to be successful.

As a result, when delivering your elevator pitch it isn't enough to establish that your Solution will be successful. You must also establish that you know how to be successful.

Unfortunately, many people are so focused on explaining their Solution that they forget to establish their own credibility.

MERELY SOLVING A PROBLEM

If you know me, then you know that I am all for solving problems. However, if you want to increase your odds of being successful, you have to remember that merely solving a problem is not enough.

Instead, you have to solve a problem that is causing people pain.

Only the existence of significant amounts of physical or psychic pain will provide the customer with the incentive they need to abandon their existing Solution and change and adopt your Solution.

IGNORING THE CUSTOMER

When it comes to products developed by engineers and other technologists, in many cases they are so focused on their Solution that they completely ignore the customer. This is a problem because spending all of your time talking about your Solution can make it look like what you are selling is a Solution In Search Of A Problem (SISOAP).

As I have learned from personal experience, the problem with a SISOAP is that finding a good problem can be an extremely time-consuming and expensive process. While large companies sometimes succeed in selling a SISOAP, they tend to be the exception that proves the rule. Most people do not have the time, and the money, it takes to find a problem that needs solving.

IGNORING THE COMPETITION

Ignoring the competition in your elevator pitch can be deadly if the audience is actually familiar with the market.

I once heard a pitch in which an entrepreneur discussed a product that would target a market with which I was extremely familiar. During his pitch he laid out a plan to do pretty much exactly what another company was doing. The entrepreneur gave no hint that he knew the competition existed, which undermined his credibility because it made me wonder if he had done his homework and really understood the market he was targeting.

People frequently ignore the competition in their elevator pitches because they are afraid that it will make their Solution look weaker when the opposite is actually true. The existence of competition can be good, because it proves that a market actually exists.

I believe one reason I had trouble getting literary agents and publishers interested in this book was the lack of direct competition. There were literally no other books that focused on creating an elevator pitch. I am sure that made some people wonder whether this was a viable market; whether enough people were interested in the subject.

In the SalesLogix elevator pitch, rather than ignoring the competition, we took on the competition directly by explaining exactly what was wrong with the state of the art...

> SalesLogix is a software company and has developed a Customer Relationship Management (CRM) system that is both easier to use and more powerful than existing solutions like Act and Siebel.

> SalesLogix is targeting mid-sized companies that have outgrown contact managers like Act but can't afford the cost and complexity of high-end CRM products like Siebel.
>
> The problem with existing CRM solutions is that they fall into one of two categories. On the one hand, you have contact managers like Act that salespeople love but that do not allow people to share information across a large organization. On the other hand you have high-end CRM systems like Siebel that scale to support the needs of hundreds or thousands of users but that salespeople refuse to use. The result is that too many organizations are unable to...
>
> - Coordinate their sales and customer service teams.
> - Obtain a holistic picture of the customer.
> - Maximize the revenue gained from each customer.

By talking about the competition and their limitations in our elevator pitch, we did two things. First, we established that we were intimately familiar with the market. Second, we explained why people would be interested in buying our product. Third, we positioned ourselves in the marketplace relative to the competition.

NOT STARTING YOUR BEST PITCHER

When it comes to the big games, baseball managers want to give the ball to their best pitcher, to their ace. They know that while that won't guarantee them a win, it will put them in the best position to win. The same thing should be true when it comes to elevator pitches, but too often it isn't.

On multiple occasions, I have worked with teams who had a Solution that stood a good chance of succeeding but who were undermined by the unwillingness of the leader of the team to delegate the delivery of the pitch to the member of the team (often the marketing person) who could best deliver the pitch. Instead, the leader of the team insisted that he (and in many cases it is a "he") be the one to deliver the pitch.

In a couple of cases, this hurt the team's efforts because the leader of the team was a technologist who didn't understand that most people weren't as interested in the HOW of his Solution as he was. In another couple of cases, the leader of the team, due to a fear of public speaking or some other anxiety, simply could not deliver the pitch in front of a large number of people.

Instead, he would absolutely lock up and end up literally not saying anything coherent.

The problem with not starting your best pitcher is that it says two things to potential investors and backers, neither of which is good. On the one hand, it says you don't understand the importance of marketing. On the other hand, it says that you don't know how to delegate.

Of course, any successful venture capitalist or management expert will tell you that understanding the importance of marketing and an ability to delegate are often the things that distinguish successful entrepreneurs from unsuccessful entrepreneurs.

As a result, if you are the leader of a team and are not a good public speaker, you have to either delegate your pitch to another member of your team or put your Solution on hold while you improve your public speaking skills.

OVER-REACHING

There is this idea going around that the only way to get the attention of a venture capitalist, angel investor, or senior executive is to characterize the opportunity for your Solution as enormous (e.g. $50 million plus). While there is some truth to that notion, in many cases people take things too far.

In one case I was listening to a series of pitches at Washington University when someone got up in front of the audience and said, "Every man, woman, and child six years old and up is in need of our technology." Another plan I once read said, "The market size for this opportunity is huge. Currently there are roughly 7 billion people on the planet."

The problem with making statements like this is that they can damage your credibility by making you look at least un-focused and in the worst case naïve. Even the largest companies do not target every person on the face of the earth right out of the gate. Instead, they target specific demographic or geographic market segments and then expand to other market segments over time.

Rather than focusing on the Theoretical Market, which is the number of people who could possibly use your product, it is better to focus on the Addressable Market, which is the number of people who definitely need your product. This is because when delivering your elevator pitch it is better for your credibility if you look focused and let the audience come to their own conclusions about the size of the Theoretical Market.

We took this tactic when selling SalesLogix. Rather than focusing on the entire CRM market, we instead focused on the middle market. Yes, we believed that SalesLogix could compete in both the high end and the low end of the market, but we thought it was more important that we put forth a plan that targeted the market segment that most obviously needed our product due to its being ignored by both our high-end and low-end competitors. Once we established ourselves in that market segment, we could then move up or down-market.

NOT SOLVING A PERSONAL PROBLEM

Over the years I have heard a number of people position their Solution in the context of broader societal trends and/or problems. Obesity and healthcare are two of the more popular ones. While this can sometimes be good, the problem is that people generally don't buy things to solve the problems of society.

Instead, people buy things to solve their own problems.

The ugly truth is that most people are generally selfish and self-centered. As a result, it rarely pays to try to solve society's problems. Instead, a much better (and more profitable) approach is to try to solve the problems of specific individuals.

If society benefits as a result, then great.

Similarly, with a few exceptions (e.g. social entrepreneurship and other non-profit ventures) investors generally don't invest in companies to solve society's problems. Instead, they invest to make money. As a result, when positioning your Solution, it is usually best to do so in the context of a specific problem that is creating a specific cost (or pain) for a specific individual or set of individuals.

CONTEMPT FOR THE AUDIENCE

Once, when reviewing a pitch that I was writing, a programmer expressed frustration with what he perceived were my efforts to "dumb down" our message. Rather impoliticly, he told me, "If they are too stupid to understand what we're doing, then I don't want to talk to them."

As I told him at the time, the problem with this attitude – which is unfortunately all too common among engineers and other technical people – is that it ignores reality. Most venture capitalists, angel investors, and senior executives are no longer, or never were, very technical. They have people who handle the low level technical details for them.

What they focus on is the general concept.

As a result, when writing your elevator pitch you must not treat the audience with contempt. Instead, you need to think like a trial lawyer. A trial lawyer cannot pick their audience. Rather, they have to take what they are given. They have to get their message across to a jury that is made up of pretty much randomly chosen people.

DIS-INTEGRATION

With very few exceptions, when I look at the one-paragraph, 100-word summaries that many entrepreneurs produce, they do not address the issue of credibility. This is a mistake because you never know how someone will first encounter your Solution. As a result, the same basic message should be conveyed, and the same topics should be addressed, in all of your marketing materials. That includes your one-paragraph summary, one-page summary, business plan, and marketing materials. I know that it can be hard and time-consuming to keep all of these documents in sync, but in my experience it is necessary because at a minimum it helps you look organized and professional.

TRYING TO CLOSE THE DEAL DURING YOUR PITCH

One reason why elevator pitches get long, and why people have a hard time cutting things out of their elevator pitches, is that people too often try to close the deal during their elevator pitch.

However, the truth is that few deals are closed without the team and the backer meeting multiple times and for many hours, during which they discuss every possible aspect of the Solution.

As a result, during your elevator pitch you should just focus on establishing WHAT you are doing, WHY you are doing it, and WHO you are. If you do that properly, and you are speaking to the correct audience, then more likely than not you will get to the next step, which is a longer, more detailed discussion of your Solution.

UNDER-REHEARSING

In national polls of the things we fear, public speaking regularly ranks up there with things like death. That's because it's incredibly hard to stand up in front of a big group of people.

I can relate to this fear because I used to feel it as well.

What I have found that helps me is being prepared and then rehearsing the heck out of my elevator pitch to the point that I can pretty much deliver it in my sleep. Before I deliver an elevator pitch to a large group of people, I have usually delivered it 25 times to an empty room and then another 75 times to individuals or small groups, which helps it become second-nature and thus builds up my confidence.

TALKING ABOUT YOUR FINANCIAL PROJECTIONS

In all my years of listening to elevator pitches, I have yet to hear someone say that they are never going to make money. As a result, in my opinion it's a waste of precious time to include things like your expected Return On Investment (ROI) or break-even point in your pitch. Instead, I believe the things you should focus on in your elevator pitch are your distinguishing factors; the things that are actually unique about you and your Solution. Experienced investors will know that your financial projections will tend to be overly positive, overly optimistic, and generally wrong. As a result, at some later point in the process they will get into the details of, and usually tear apart, your financial model.

INTRODUCING EACH TEAM MEMBER BY NAME

Quite frequently, presenters will introduce each member of their team during the course of their pitch. In most cases, I find this to be a waste of precious time because the people who are mentioned don't bring anything special or unique to the team. Instead, they are just playing a role (e.g. the marketing guy or the finance person).

A good rule of thumb to follow is that unless a person has a significant amount of extremely relevant experience, there is usually no need to introduce them during your elevator pitch. Instead, it is enough to just mention how much total relevant experience you have among the team as a whole. That is the approach we took with the SalesLogix elevator pitch...

> *The SalesLogix team has over 75 years of combined experience in the industry and is led by Pat Sullivan, the co-founder and former CEO of Contact Software International, the original developer of Act.*

We mentioned Pat Sullivan by name because he was the leader of the team and had significant credibility as a result of his past accomplishments. We just lumped together everyone else's experience and only named names during our investor presentation and in our business plan.

6. BEFORE'S AND AFTER'S

> *"The most valuable of all talents is that of never using two words when one will do."*
> – Thomas Jefferson

In conducting elevator pitch seminars and workshops, I have found that one of the most valuable things I do is when I go through elevator pitches, explaining what's wrong with them, and explaining what I would change, and why. As a result, on the following pages I discuss some elevator pitches I have developed for companies I have either worked for or with. These include...

- **Care Coordinator**
- **Novel Imaging**
- **Rogue Research**

In each case, the revised elevator pitch improved the team's ability to communicate their message and had a measurable impact on their sales, marketing, and fundraising efforts.

6.1. CARECOORDINATOR

> *"If you can't write your idea on the back of my calling card, you don't have a clear idea."*
> – David Belasco

I first met the CareCoordinator team while coaching the teams who were participating in Washington University's Olin Cup business plan competition. When I initially heard their elevator pitch, it went like this...

> CareCoordinator is a service company with web-based information management software that captures homecare case information, connects family caregivers and independent case managers, and enables users to share information to manage on-site and long-distance homecare.
>
> There is currently no other product that combines these features. By filling this niche, CareCoordinator will enhance communication between individual family members and service agencies so that homecare can be managed more effectively, resulting in less hardship on caregivers and improved care for older adults.
>
> We are an aging society. Older Americans with chronic conditions are living longer. The older we get, the more likely we are to require assistance with activities of daily living (ADL's). Over 50% of individuals age 84 or older commonly require assistance with their daily activities. Family caregivers are traditionally the ones who provide this assistance; of these, 60% are between the ages of 36 and 65 and 64% have full-time jobs. CareCoordinator will be distributed through licenses to:
>
> • **Business HR departments and employee assistance programs.** American businesses lose an estimated $20 billion each year due to lost productivity from employees who are helping a family member live at home.

- **Family caregiver households.** There are 14 million caregiver households in the U.S., with over 200,000 in the St. Louis metropolitan service area.

- **Family members who provide long-distance care for relatives.** There are seven million family members who provide long-distance care to an elderly or disabled loved one. They need access to daily status information and resources so that they can take action even when they are not in the home.

- **Hospitals and healthcare providers.** For example, Patrick Lee, CEO of Rusk Rehabilitation Center, understands the benefits that CareCoordinator offers and wants to be among the first to utilize it for outpatients.

- **Independent case managers and service agencies.** There is currently little or no connection between family and professional caregivers in 80% of homecare cases.

- **Government agencies,** e.g. Mid-East or St. Louis Area Agencies on Aging.

- **Non-profit organizations who provide assistance to older adults,** e.g. the Alzheimer's Association.

Families can open an account from the website for $100. Or, for the same amount they could open their account through a local care manager who will visit them, provide advice, and help them set it up or she can set it up for them if they live far away. Through the Internet, family members can access current information with professional involvement to help them make decisions, develop a plan and manage changes. We will discount the semi-annual fee to professionals, corporations, and non-profits. We have a strong team experienced in providing services to older adult populations.

We need $87,000 to develop a pilot that we will present to corporations and VC to find the $6 million we need for start-up. Our goals are to average $20,000 a day in sales by our second year and serve over 100,000 customers. Our investors will receive a highly competitive ROI and participate in the selection of the people who will operate and grow the company.

If you evaluate the initial CareCoordinator elevator pitch in terms of The Nine C's, you will see that there were a number of fundamental problems with it.

First, the initial CareCoordinator elevator pitch was not at all concise. Instead, at 506 words it was much too long. As a result, they were not able to deliver the pitch in two minutes (only the guy in the early FedEx commercials could).

What's more, in trying to rush through their pitch, the team looked hurried and frazzled, which damaged their credibility.

Second, the initial CareCoordinator elevator pitch wasn't as clear as it could be. While it was led off by a summary sentence, the list of seven possible target markets made it hard to figure out exactly WHO the customer was. What's more, and worse, it made them look unfocused.

Third, instead of being conceptual, the CareCoordinator elevator pitch spent much too much time discussing the HOW of the idea and not enough time discussing exactly WHAT they were trying to do and WHY.

Finally, the initial version of the CareCoordinator elevator pitch didn't mention who made up the team, so they never established their credibility. They never explained why they would be able to do what they wanted to do.

After getting to know the leader of the team, we came up with this revised version...

> My name is Hal Oliver and my company, CareCoordinator, is developing an online management tool that helps families and caregivers coordinate homecare efforts and enables older adults to remain in their homes.
>
> A few years ago, I owned a private pay, private duty homecare business. One problem I frequently came across during this time was adult children who were trying to care for their aging parents from a distance or while working full time. They were constantly at risk of losing their jobs because of their need to make phone calls, take unplanned leaves, and reschedule business trips in order to take care of their parents.
>
> What adults with aging parents need is a tool that will enable them to set up and access home-care information, take advantage of local professional care managers, and help them make decisions, develop plans, and manage changes.
>
> CareCoordinator's initial target market will be large corporations with employee assistance programs.

> The CareCoordinator team is experienced in providing services to older adult populations. Our team includes a professional care manager, a social worker with expertise in using Internet technology to advance social work practices, a marketing expert, and a president of an older adult education and volunteer service organization.
>
> CareCoordinator needs $87,000 to develop a prototype that we will present to corporations and Venture Capitalists and that will help us raise the $6 million we need to solve one of the greatest problems of the 21st century; the care and well-being of our aging population.

The revised CareCoordinator elevator pitch was much more consistent with The Nine C's and as a result was much more effective.

First, and most obviously, the revised CareCoordinator elevator pitch was much more concise; at 249 words, it was only half as long. This meant it could be delivered at a much more measured pace, which helped the presenter and the team look more credible.

Second, to help establish the credibility of the team, the revised Care Coordinator elevator pitch very explicitly established the experience the team had with the problem. It turned out that the CareCoordinator had a significant amount of credibility that they never mentioned in the original version of their elevator pitch.

Finally, the revised CareCoordinator elevator pitch was more conceptual. It spent more time talking about the problem they were trying to solve and their experience dealing with it. This also helped to bolster their credibility.

6.2. NOVEL IMAGING

> "If it takes a lot of words to say what you have in mind, give it more thought."
> – Dennis Roth

I also met the Novel Imaging team while coaching the teams who were participating in Washington University's Olin Cup business plan competition. When I first heard Novel Imaging's elevator pitch, it started out like this...

> Novel Imaging is an early stage company dedicated to the discovery, development and commercialization of radiotracers and radioligands for applications in Single Photon Emission Computed Tomography (SPECT) and Positron Emission Tomography (PET) imaging.
>
> Near term commercialization focuses on the radioactive isotope Copper-64 (64Cu) for applications in PET Imaging and therapy and targeted tumor imaging of sigma-2 receptors by way of proprietary ligands. The first ligand would be a sigma-2 receptor ligand labeled with Tc-99m for breast, lung and head & neck tumors. Longer-term efforts for sigma-2 receptor ligands will focus on measuring the proliferative status (growth and spread) of tumor cells.
>
> The company will be led by Michael Bronowicz, an individual with 9 years of management experience in Nuclear Medicine. Mr. Bronowicz managed the global Nuclear Medicine business unit at Mallinckrodt Medical. The business unit achieved M$300 in sales revenue under his leadership. Inventors of the technologies, Dr. Michael Welch and Dr. Robert Mach will support management as scientific advisors to the company. Michael J. Welch, Ph.D., is an internationally known researcher and leader in the field of nuclear medicine. He is Director of the Division of Radiation Sciences at Mallinckrodt Institute of Radiology (MIR). His research in the field of P.E.T. imaging has led to a number of

patents related to radioisotope manufacturing, target preparation and ligand design. Robert H. Mach, Ph.D., is Director of the P.E.T. Scan Center at Mallinckrodt Institute of Radiology. His research has focused on the application of radiotracers in both PET and SPECT imaging studies of tumors.

Novel Imaging's proprietary technology platform is based on several inventions. Technology related to Copper-64 and other isotopes is based on a patented method of production of the isotopes. The availability of isotopes manufactured by this method is limited currently to one site, MIR. Clinical grade material suitable for use in preparing radiodiagnostic-imaging agents is currently being manufactured and shipped to over thirty facilities in the USA. These customers will soon be supplied by Novel Imaging, which will result in an immediate revenue stream for the company. Revenues for the first 5 years are expected to be around M$7.0. Sigma-2 expression has been shown to correlate with cell proliferation (growth and spread) in tumors. A radiolabeled sigma-2 ligand could be used to image tumors and predict their response to radiation therapy and chemotherapy. The technology platform focused on sigma-2 receptors provides novel radiolabeled sigma-2 ligands for use in the diagnosis of tumors. Our proprietary compounds are also suitable for noninvasive methods that may accurately assess the proliferative status of cancer cells in breast, lung and head & neck tumors. The company is expected to take this technology into human clinical trials, focused on breast cancer initially, within 12 months of the commencement of operations. Advances in MIR, CT, Ultrasound, SPECT and PET equipment design and enhancements drive competition for tumor imaging. There are also several radiopharmaceutical agents under development that will require human clinical trials and FDA approval. Our sigma-2 receptor agent will be focused initially on the detection of breast tumors in women with dense tissue, breast implants and scarring as a result of biopsy. This patient type is not well served by mammography. Both thick breast tissue and breast cancer tumors appear as white regions on a mammogram film, which can cause dense breast tissue, implants and scarring to eclipse the cancer. We expect to penetrate the breast tumor market by 3% resulting in first year sales of M$20.

Novel Imaging has key patents, proprietary know-how, and licensing agreements under negotiations with Washington University and Wake Forest University. In addition, Novel Imaging's inventors continue to identify development opportunities that define noninvasive methods that may accurately assess the proliferative status of cancer cells in breast, lung and head & neck tumors and predict the response of these types of tumors to radiation therapy and chemotherapy.

Novel Imaging is seeking K$200 to commence operations. First year revenues of K$480 from the sale of Copper-64 will supplement initial funding. Funding will be used for payroll/benefits, travel, office rent/lease and overhead, legal support and to initiate toxicology studies for the sigma-2 receptor technology. Funding and revenues are expected to last 9 months.

Funding for sigma-2 human clinical trials in the range of M$1.7-2.2 will be required to initiate and complete trials thru Phase 2 (IND, Phase 1, and Phase 2). In addition, revenues from copper-64 will be used to supplement company operations.

The company will seek partners for isotope production and distribution. Interest in the sigma-2 receptor ligand, as an adjunct to therapy, would be expected to come from major pharmaceutical companies currently focused on the treatment of cancer.

The Novel Imaging management team will consist of the President/CEO and later in the first year a Chief Scientific Officer (CSO). A CFO and a laboratory scientist will be added in the second year. Accounting, legal, regulatory, etc. will be outsourced. Guidance and support from the two inventors will insure transfer of technical knowledge and commercialization of the ongoing operation.

The company exit strategy would be to position itself as an acquisition or merger candidate for pharmaceutical or imaging equipment companies interested in access to technical expertise in isotope production and ligand design and development.

The company is currently seeking both corporate and science advisory board members who can provide expertise in the financial, medical (focus on cancer) and strategic planning functions.

There were obviously a number of problems with this version of the Novel Imaging elevator pitch.

First, at 891 words this version of the Novel Imaging elevator pitch was much too long. As a result, it took forever to deliver.

Second, this version of the Novel Imaging elevator pitch used too much jargon. It was absolutely packed with acronyms and scientific terms that very few Ordinary People could understand. This limited the number of people who could understand the pitch.

Third, this version of the Novel Imaging elevator pitch was a perfect example of a worm burner; an elevator pitch that gets too detailed too quickly. There was too much unnecessary, low-level detail in this version of the Novel Imaging elevator pitch. In part, this was because the team seemed to be trying to close the deal with their elevator pitch rather than just trying to get to the next conversation.

Finally, this version of the Novel Imaging elevator pitch didn't answer the "So what?" question. There was no discussion of the benefits of all those big, fancy, technical words. At no point did the Novel Imaging team explain why the world needed a product that could do what they said it could.

After spending some time talking to the leader of the Novel Imaging team, we came up with this revised version of their elevator pitch...

> *Novel Imaging is a life sciences company dedicated to the discovery and development of products that will enable physicians to detect and treat tumors in their earliest stages.*
>
> *When it comes to screening for breast cancer, existing detection systems like mammography have a difficult time discriminating between cancerous tissue and tissue that is dense, covered by an implant, or the result of scarring. As a result, 25% of the mammography exams done each year result in women being told that they have an abnormality on their mammography and need to undergo biopsies, ultrasound and other follow-up tests, only to find that they do not have breast cancer.*
>
> *Novel Imaging has developed a product that, when injected into the body, attaches itself to the wall of any cancer cells that are present in breast tissue and will highlight both the size and location of the cancerous growth.*
>
> *Mike Bronowicz, President & CEO, has been involved in the manufacturing, distribution, marketing and sales of medical products for the past 25 years. The inventors of our technology, Dr. Michael Welch and Dr. Robert Mach are located at Mallinckrodt Institute of Radiology. Both scientists are internationally known researchers and leaders in the field of Nuclear Medicine.*

> *The company is seeking $500,000 to move to the next phase of operations. Expected revenues of $480,000 from another product line that the company has licensed will be combined with initial funding and will be used for product development.*

The revised Novel Imaging elevator pitch did a much better job of explaining who they were and what they were trying to accomplish.

First, this version of the Novel Imaging elevator pitch started off with a short summary sentence, which set the stage for what followed. It gave the listener a basic sense of where the rest of the pitch was going, which made it easier for the audience to follow along.

Second, this version of the Novel Imaging elevator pitch was very explicit when it came to identifying the problem and answering the "So what?" question. Where they had previously spent too much time getting into all of the details of HOW their Solution worked, in this version of their elevator pitch they steered clear of issues of HOW and instead focused on answering the WHAT and WHY questions.

Third, the revised Novel Imaging elevator pitch did a much better job of highlighting the credibility of the team. Where before the background of the founders – which was quite strong – was buried in the middle of the pitch, in this version it was toward the end of the pitch where it stood out better.

6.3. ROGUE RESEARCH

> *"Whoever knows he is deep, strives for clarity; whoever would like to appear deep to the crowd, strives for obscurity."*
>
> – Nietzsche

I joined Rogue Research[7] when they were nearing the completion of the initial development of their product and were starting to look for people to market both the product and the company. Prior to my joining the company, they were using this elevator pitch ...

> Rogue Research is revolutionizing the way in which large-scale, mission critical applications will be delivered and deployed. Cloud technology from Rogue Research is architected for order of magnitude improvements in cost and performance characteristics. Much like workers in a bee-hive, a Rogue Cloud brings together up to several hundred thousand workers into a single, high-availability computing environment perfect for delivering mission-critical applications. When compared with current approaches, applications developed with Rogue technology are significantly more available (Cloud-based applications have no reason to ever go down), significantly more scalable (capable of growing from a handful of CPUs to hundreds of thousands of processing elements), are inexpensive to maintain (all members of a Cloud are always administered as a single system, no matter how large or complex), and require at least 90% less capital to acquire. Multiple Clouds may be clustered or spread geographically, and can be linked to existing computing facilities.

As soon as I joined the company, and started talking to people and judging whether this version of the Rogue Research elevator pitch was effective, it quickly became clear that there were a number of problems with it.

First, this version of the Rogue Research elevator pitch was much too complex. All of those parenthetical statements made it hard to deliver, much less listen too. To a large degree, this version of the Rogue Research elevator pitch assumed the audience was going to read or listen carefully to what we had to say. That didn't turn out to be a valid assumption. At that time we were raising money from angel investors and this elevator pitch generally just left them confused. They couldn't figure out what it was that we did or made. They also couldn't figure out what type of company we were; whether we were a hardware company or a software company.

As a result, they generally tuned us out quickly.

A second weakness of this version of the Rogue Research elevator pitch was that it focused on the technology and pretty much ignored the product and the customer. This wasn't surprising, given that the company was founded and run by engineers. However, while engineers love to think and talk about technologies, at the end of the day Ordinary People buy products and solutions, not raw technologies.

Finally, the biggest problem with this version of the Rogue Research elevator pitch was that it did not highlight the credibility of the team. This was a problem for two reasons. First, what we were doing was cutting edge and risky. As a result, the credibility of the team was a major consideration. Second, one of the things we had a ton of was credibility. The heart of the team was made up of people who had built another succesful product and company. However, the initial version of the Rogue Research elevator pitch never mentioned that critical fact.

After coming on board and familiarizing myself with what we had to sell, I developed a new elevator pitch that went like this...

> *Rogue Research has developed a software product, called Cloud Creator, which enables businesses and other organizations to simultaneously reduce the cost, and improve the reliability, of mission critical applications.*
>
> *Cloud Creator enables large numbers of commodity computers to join together and form a self-organizing, self-healing, and self-managing system called a Cloud. A Cloud is more survivable, more scalable, and more affordable than existing solutions like fault tolerant computers and application servers.*
>
> *Rogue Research is led by _____ , former co-founder and CEO of _____ , which was acquired by _____ in 2000 in a deal valued at more than $100 million.*

This new version of the Rogue Research elevator pitch worked much better for a number of reasons.

First, it put the focus on the product, not the technology. We did this because venture capitalists are usually reluctant to finance, and customers are reluctant to take a risk on, raw technologies because they can take so long to develop.

Instead, they prefer products that are close to shipping.

Second, this version of the Rogue Research elevator pitch retained a fairly technical flavor. This was because we were in the process of recruiting business partners and were interested in attracting the attention of both investors and geeks. As a result, it was important that we maintained a technical edge to our pitch. However, this version of the elevator pitch did a better job of making clear both the features and the benefits of the product.

Third, this version of the Rogue Research elevator pitch was very concise. While we could expand it if necessary to fill time, this version of our elevator pitch got our most important points across while explicitly establishing the credibility of the team.

7. CODA

RECOMMENDED READING

If you want to learn more about how to be an effective communicator, and why it's so important, I recommend that you read the following books...

The 22 Immutable Laws of Marketing, Al Ries & Jack Trout
How to Get Your Point Across in 30 Seconds or Less, Milo O. Frank
Presenting to Win, Jerry Weissman

If you want to see how some great writers communicate complex, technical subjects in a way that is understandable by Ordinary People, I recommend that you take a look at the following books...

The Dinosaur Heresies, Robert Baaker
A Short History of Nearly Everything, Bill Bryson
Why Zebras Don't Get Ulcers, Robert Sapolsky

You should also consider reading any of the 20 or so books by Stephen Jay Gould that contain some of his essays that were published in Natural History magazine.

ACKNOWLEDGEMENTS

While my name is the one that's on the cover, this book reflects the collective wisdom of a much larger community.

The genesis of this book was a problem that a friend of mine named Gary Langenfeld had and a conversation that we had as a result. During that conversation, he encouraged me to write this book. That conversation then led to a series of critical discussions with Mark Lewis, a friend of mine who is also a venture capitalist. Over the years, and thanks to a series of experiences that were facilitated by Ken Harrington at Washington University, I was able to flesh out this book and turn it into what it is today.

Of course, Gary, Mark, and Ken weren't the only people who helped me bring this book to life. Over the years I was helped, influenced, and encouraged by a large number of other people, including Shante Redding, Chris Dornfeld, Andrea Reubin, Kristin Daugherty, and Rosemary Gliedt at Washington University in St. Louis and a number of other people both in St. Louis and around the country including Gil Bickel, Mike Bronowitz, Guy Kawasaki, Bill Meade, Geoff Moore, James S. O'Rourke IV, Al Ries, Russ Roberts, Bill Simon, Pat Sullivan, Tom Walsh, Mike Wilcox, and Carter Williams. I would like to thank my team of proofreaders, which includes Mary Ellen Sliment, Cyndee Sullivan, and Doug and Kathie O'Leary. I would also like to thank my stellar graphic designer, Katie Robinson.

Finally, I'd like to thank country singer Kenny Chesney for his song *No Shoes, No Shirt, No Problems* which kept me focused and motivated while I was straining to finish this book.

ENDNOTES

1. The SalesLogix elevator pitch, positioning and marketing materials, and overall strategy were heavily influenced by Al Ries. It was an honor to work with and get to know one of the great minds in marketing and advertising.

2. Thanks to Mark Lewis for suggesting the analogy that an elevator pitch is like an accordion.

3. For much more detail on the difference between Experts and Ordinary People, see Geoffrey Moore's excellent *Crossing The Chasm* and Everett M. Rogers' seminal *Diffusion of Innovations*.

4. There are exceptions to this rule. Some people seem to revel in change. However, if you look at their lives in detail, in general they will tend to resist most changes. Yes, they may go to a different restaurant every weekend, but they resist change in other parts of their lives.

5. I explain the relationship between pain, change, and innovation in depth in my forthcoming book *The Paradox of Pain*.

6. You shouldn't expect a professional venture capitalist to sign a Non-Disclosure Agreement (NDA). This isn't a problem because professional venture capitalists know that if they were to make public a certain piece of confidential information then their reputation would be ruined.

7. The name of this company has been disguised.